This book is filled with terms, reports and everything I
needed for my small business needs.
— Famous person

QUICKBOOKS

Small Business Bookkeeping and Accounting Guide

The Best QuickBooks Pocket Guide for Successful Small Businesses

Second Edition

Presented By

The Preneur's Guide

Authored By

Zachary Weiner

Third Avenue Publishing LLC
157 E. 86th St. #506
New York, NY, 10028
info@thirdavenuepublishing.com

ISBN-13: 978-0692178218 (paperback)
ISBN-10: 069217821X (paperback)

Ordering Information:
Quantity sales. Special discounts are available on quantity purchases by corporations, associations, and others. For details, contact the publisher at the address above.

This book is dedicated to the people in my life (you know who you are) who refused to give up on me and my wild dreams.

Contents

Introduction

Business is hard, no question about that. Whether you are a solopreneur, a small business owner, or a large business owner, the challenges are truly endless—from marketing and sales, to human resources and financial reporting. Of course, in reality, these challenges come with personal and financial freedoms that cannot be achieved working for someone else. Ask any business owner if they could see themselves working under another owner—an overwhelming number say no!

This book does not serve as an all-inclusive guide to business and finance. A book of that nature would be endless, as new questions arise daily from various industries. This small book serves instead as a starting guide, a framework for the small business owner to better understand and report their financials using one of the most popular software program currently on the market—QuickBooks.

Software changes rapidly. As I am writing this book, there have already been significant changes in the QuickBooks Online reports feature. Despite these changes, the rationale for QuickBooks-based accounting and the approaches to it described in the pages below will continue to be relevant. Focus on absorbing the large themes, as these will guide you in the direction you hope to take—financial and accounting success.

I personally despise introductions, so let's get into what you came here to read. Over the coming pages, you will be educated on the most popular accounting software with the goal of making endless challenges easier to handle.

Chapter 1

Why Account At All?

Why Account At All?

You may ask yourself why you should account at all: Why do I need to track what is going on in my business? Without understanding and capably navigating accounting terms and reports you won't be able to succeed in the long term. Accounting is the basic framework of a business. I'm sure you have heard of the terms: profit and loss, cost of goods sold, gross profit, return on investment. But these and many other terms may sound foreign and overwhelming.

At the end of the year, when your CPA requests your balance sheet, income statement, and statement of cash flows, do you avoid returning the email? For the lucky few of you who have business partners who've invested capital, it becomes even more challenging because you might feel that your partners are talking a different language. Quarterly or monthly investment meetings centered around the language of business just aren't an easy or productive experience for a novice. You may not be well-versed in what those terms are and what those reports mean, so to imagine yourself working within QuickBooks seems impossible.

Pause: In the coming pages we will cover all those challenging terms and more. More importantly, each term will be explained in plain English so you can make solid financial decisions based on accurate financials. Knowledge of terms will make your business meetings more productive and the ability to make sound financial decisions much more attainable.

Accounting is not a recent development. It has been around since the Romans marked their stone tablets with notches for their number of sheep. In fact, you probably learned all the basic accounting tools necessary for success in grade school. Understanding the goals of accounting will allow you to better reach your business objectives. Accounting serves two main purposes:

1. To educate you, the business owner, on what is going on in your business
2. To help you report your business operations to the tax authorities

It's really just that simple.

Let's dive a bit deeper.

Why Educate Yourself?

Why would you want to educate yourself about your business? This may seem like an odd and idiotic question—why would you need to know more about your business, like come on, it's YOUR business? Looking at your business and its goals through the lens of accounting will give you a fresh perspective and allow you to make better decisions. Educating yourself about your business is really the main point of financial reporting. Budgets allow you to set business goals for you and your team. Financial reports allow you to see if you have met the goals you set for yourself. Reporting allows you to highlight points where you fell short or missed the mark. Key performance indicators (KPIs for short) allow you to measure your business against others within your industry to see how you stand.

Through education, you can make better decisions. Better decisions result in a better business. And we all know a better business results in a better life for our family and sounder sleep at night. Instead of thinking about financials as some incomprehensible chicken scratch that only the MBAs can understand, think about it as a mentor to help guide your business to success. Similarly, the time-tested accounting principles have led businesses to success for hundreds of years. Today's accounting software is both user-friendly and time effective. These accounting principles will serve as your mentors in helping your business grow or consolidate to ensure that you profit in the best way possible.

Many big questions come to mind for a small business operation: Should I hire another staff member? Do I make money on this product? Should I focus on x part of my business? Should I offer free shipping? Do I charge enough for my product or services?

QuickBooks has these answers hidden within it, and they are there for the taking. The next few chapters will help you pull those answers out.

Thoroughly understanding these financial reports and key metrics will give you the answers you are searching for. Complex questions will be able to be seen in a yes-or-no format. Key margins can be calculated with simple division, and profitability will be available as a percentage of revenue.

Why Report Your Business?

The IRS and state governments want to know what you do. The state wants to know how many items you sell, if your business made any money, if you personally made money, and how much you paid in taxes. The IRS wants to know how and in what format you made or lost money. Whatever political beliefs you harbor, the government requires you to pay sales and income taxes, and QuickBooks helps you do just that.

The expression is timeless and truly annoying: "But in this world nothing can be said to be certain, except death and taxes." In America, one cannot get through life without the two. No matter your political affiliation or how you feel about paying your earnings or profit to the government, taxes are unavoidable. The risks greatly outweigh the slight benefits of avoiding paying a small share of your earnings to the government.

By understanding how to correctly track expenses and account for items, such as sales tax, you can ensure you remain compliant and never fear the wrath of the IRS or state governments. By accounting properly for large equipment purchases, leasehold improvement, store buildouts, etc., you can ensure you take the proper deductions for years to come. We will touch on the proper accounting procedures for those items later on.

Chapter 2

A Short History Lesson

History of Accounting

Every university offers semester-long lectures on the history of business and/or the history of accounting. In that course, professors lecture about how accounting has been around since things needed to be counted (i.e., when the Romans marked their stone tablets with notches for their number of sheep). Accounting in the form we see it today has been around since states or nations needed to report finances to the king or ruler. The basis of accounting is to report accurate financial information.

Accounting in the form of double entry, the format popular in our current society, was really popularized in the late fifteenth century by Luca Pacioli. He was the first to document the world of double accounting and much more in a legible written format. To be honest, he changed our interpretation of accounting as we know it and that of algebra (yes, his famous book outlined the basics of algebra, too). As I previously mentioned, the math you learned in grade school is all you need to account properly.

I won't bore you with a semester-long history lesson here, but the fact is that Luca documented the basic accounting principles of today. It was the idea that everything should be accounted for or have an entry. He had a ledger that included assets such as inventory and receivables, liabilities, cash, income, and expenses. He even went so far as to suggest that one should not sleep if all the numbers did not tie. He is widely considered the father of accounting and even provided year-end closing entries (something today's CPAs regularly supply).

The Story Behind the QuickBooks Rise to Fame

Back in the 80s, accounting software was overwhelming and tedious. When you did double entry accounting, you had to do two entries: Hence the term *double entry*. You had to credit and debit the right accounts and know all the tricks of the trade. Those of you who took that business course back in college may remember those miserable debit and credit lectures. (Or more likely you remember the fantastic naps you had at 9:00 a.m. Mondays, Wednesdays, and Fridays.)

During the 80s, Intuit—the makers of QuickBooks— came out with a product that eliminated the need for double entry. Intuit realized that small business owners were busy running their business and not researching the intricacies of double-entry accounting. It took a few different versions before the elite accounting world accepted the product, but it quickly grew to over 80 percent market share of the accounting software for small businesses.

QuickBooks made accounting software more approachable and user-friendly. It allowed business owners to take control of their businesses and has empowered these small business owners ever since. Simultaneous with the rise of tools for small business was growth in small business and solo entrepreneurship.

Decades ago, even 10 or 20 years ago, a startup or new small business would have required a brick and mortar shop and the ability to distribute goods or services in-house, but today all that is needed is some form of a workplace (like a couch in the living room), a laptop, and internet access. This change in both the barriers to entry as well as the tools available for new business owners has reshaped the business landscape.

QuickBooks and other Intuit software programs are designed to make your business life easier. Think of QuickBooks as a tool, like your email or your smartphone, that allows you to connect with customers, employees, partners, and business owners all over the world and that helps you solve problems all hours of the day.

Chapter 3

The Language of Accounting

Why All These Funny Words?

Oftentimes industry professionals develop their own language. Initially the idea behind this was likely to communicate better with peers. But it has turned into a barrier to entry—confusing terms and analogies with the goal of keeping outsiders out.

Do you need to pay a professional $500 or more an hour if you can figure out the answers to the questions yourself? No, you do not need a high-level professional for much of what is going on in your business. You just need to better understand the terms and the associated ideas behind them.

The List!

Accounts Payable

Accounts payable (A/P) is the amount a business owes its suppliers or creditors. Oftentimes these are debts that must be paid off within a given period to avoid default. On many company's balance sheets, accounts payable is often logged as a current liability.

The payable is essentially a short-term IOU from one business to another business, which acts as a creditor.

Accounts Receivable

Accounts receivable (A/R) is the amount a business is owed by its customers. This number fluctuates over the course of the business and should be reviewed often. On your company's balance sheet, accounts receivable is often logged as a current asset.

Accrual Basis Accounting

Accrual Basis Accounting refers to one of the two major accounting methods. Accrual Basis Accounting is a method that records revenues and expenses when they are incurred, regardless of when cash is received or disbursed. The term *accrual* refers to any individual entry recording revenue or expense in the absence of a cash transaction. One example of this would be invoicing a customer but not yet receiving payment—the invoice is recorded as revenue but the cash transaction has yet to occur. Another example would be entering an expense invoice before payment has been remitted—this is considered an expense based on the date of services, not payment.

Asset

An asset is any resource of economic value that a company owns. Yes, your truck is an asset if owned by the company. The money you used to build out the fixtures and furnishing in your store is an asset. The computer equipment that sits on your desk is an asset. So on and so forth.

Balance Sheet

A company's balance sheet gives a snapshot of the company's financial health in a given moment. This includes the cash it has on hand, bank account balances, the liabilities it has outstanding, and equity the owners have in the business.

Bottom Line

This is the total amount a business has made or lost at the end of a given period. The reference to *bottom* describes the relative location of the net income on a company's income statement. The term can also be used in the context of a business's earnings increasing or decreasing.

Cash Basis Accounting

Cash basis refers to the other major accounting method. This approach recognizes revenues and expenses at the time physical cash is actually received or paid out. When transactions are recorded on a cash basis, they affect a company's books only once a completed exchange of value has occurred; therefore, cash basis accounting is less accurate than accrual accounting in the short term.

Cash Flow

Cash flow is usually defined by investors as being the key metric to a firm's financial health. Cash flow is really the difference between what you report on your financial statements that is not cash and cash transactions that actually occur.

In the accrual method of accounting, you are allowed to count your chickens before they hatch. This means that you can record money coming in and expenses leaving before the physical cash transaction actually occurs. For example, when you create an invoice, the sale has occurred, but really do you have the money yet? No! Cash flow reverses out all these items and gives you a true understanding of your real dollars in hand. Eliminating invoices billed to customers and expenses entered that are not yet paid—showing you the real cash transactions in your business.

This is oftentimes displayed in a statement of cash flows.

Debt

Similar to your house mortgage, a debt is money owed on an asset. It can also be merely money owed by the business. A debt in business could mean a loan, a line of credit, or money you borrowed from your mother. Better keep these debts in check to make sure your business stays healthy.

Depreciation

Large expenditures, such as the purchase of a vehicle or building, will add value to the business over an extended period. Accrual accounting treats these purchases differently and will make them an expense over their usable life. For example, a vehicle will likely serve your business for seven years, so you will take an annual expense for this vehicle over seven years. Over time, a business's assets decrease in value due to the time that has passed since they were purchased. For tax purposes, a business can recover the cost of that depreciation through a deduction. Consult with your CPA to set a depreciation schedule and ensure you are depreciating all your assets correctly.

Equity and Owners Equity

In the simplest of terms, equity is assets minus liabilities. An owner's equity is typically explained in terms of the percentage ownership or stock a person or entity has ownership interest in in the company.

Expenses

Business expenses are the costs the company incurs in order to operate. These are such things as rent, utilities, professional and legal fees, employee wages, contractor pay, and marketing and advertising costs.

Liability

Liability is simply an obligation to repay debt. Oftentimes this is similar to a loan or line of credit. But a liability goes a bit farther and can be sales tax you owe the government or payroll taxes you owe the state.

Net Income

In the most basic sense, net income means a company's total earnings or profit. You start with income, money from the sales of services or goods. Then, you minus out COGS, an expense for creating the previously mentioned sales or goods. You next minus out everything else you spent money on—such as gas for the truck, a manager to run the store, etc. All that is left (which I hope for your sake is a lot) is your net income.

P.S. An increase in net income is usually a good thing!

Net Worth

Net worth refers to assets minus liability, used by both companies and individuals. A continual increase in net worth indicates good financial health; conversely, net worth may be depleted by business losses.

Profit and Loss (income statement)

Also known as a profit and loss statement, an income statement shows the profitability of a business during a period of time. The income statement looks at a business's revenues, cost of goods, and expenses through all of its activities (including all bank accounts, credit cards, etc.).

Chapter 4

Which QuickBooks is Right for You?

QuickBooks for Mac

Who's It For?

This is a bit obvious, but this product is for Mac users. With the many keyboard tricks integrated into the Mac operating system, QuickBooks for Mac enables the user to reach optimum efficiency.

Where Does It Live?

The QuickBooks files and applications live on your Mac. The company file can be stored on an external hard drive, but to ensure that you do not corrupt the file, it is best to have this stored on your Mac.

What Features Are Included?

All the features you would expect from a desktop version of QuickBooks are included. For an extra fee, the file can be hosted in the cloud, allowing access from multiple Mac computers located at different locations.

What Features Are Forgotten?

Cloud hosting and automatic updates are not included in the version for Mac desktops. Additionally, you are limited to access by only three users, so it has potential to limit you as you grow your small business.

What's It Cost?

The real cost of the software is $299 per year, but it also requires an annual support contract of $299 that recurs yearly.

Is It User-Friendly?

What is great about the Mac for QuickBooks is that it is built for Macs. QuickBooks for Macs make use of Mac keyboard shortcuts, and as an avid Mac user myself, I know that keyboard shortcuts save time (and thus money)!

What Else Do You Need to Know About This Software?

Of all of the desktop versions of QuickBooks, the Mac version is the least robust. As your business grows and you need a more advanced version of QuickBooks, you will be all but forced to move to the PC version. QuickBooks Pro, QuickBooks Premier, and QuickBooks Enterprise are PC-based systems, so it may be best to focus your energies on setting yourself up the right way from the get-go to save you headaches down the line.

Final Thoughts

This product is for a Mac addict. If you can live without your Mac, go with one of the other versions listed below.

QuickBooks Online

Who's It For?

QuickBooks Online is designed for anyone to access. You can access the same file from a PC, Mac, or even from your smartphone (yes, you can even code your bank feed from your smartphone). Simply put, QuickBooks Online allows access from all your computer devices.

Where Does It Live?

The file lives in the world of Intuit (the QuickBooks parent company). It is likely on an Amazon server either in Virginia or Northern California, depending on your location. In layman's terms, it lives in the cloud.

What Features Are Included?

All of the basic QuickBooks features are included. This ranges from customers, journal entries, bank feeds, bank reconciliations, and so on. Some of the more advanced features that Pro, Premier, and Enterprise users might expect are not included.

What Features Are Forgotten?

All of the robust find features, advanced sorting features, and a lot of other features considered the norm for the desktop products are missing. Business owners who have used the desktop products for years often find the transition to QBO very difficult.

What's It Cost?

The online version is comparable to the desktop versions. It starts at $20 per month, which comes out to about $240 annually. If you prefer more features, such as the ability to send estimates, have multiple users, and track inventory—the price will increase.

Is It User-Friendly?

QuickBooks Online is like all software-as-a-service products you would experience in today's world. A software-as-a-service product is an application, like one on your smart phone, where both the software and the data are provided to a customer for a reoccurring fee. The user interface is friendly and fairly simple. Overall, the software is simpler and easier to navigate from the start.

What Else Do You Need to Know About This Software?

This QuickBooks Online software is really designed for a small business owner just starting out. If you have one stream of revenue, a few bills, and a small list of expenses, this is the perfect software for you. It also allows for you to pay monthly versus a larger upfront fee.

Final Thoughts

QuickBooks Online is very solid small business accounting software. If this is your first foray into small business accounting, it will give you all you need. If you have multiple profit centers, need complex invoicing, and plan on having a few staff members in your accounting departments—the products that follow are best for you.

QuickBooks Pro

Who's It For?

QuickBooks Desktop Pro is the most basic of the PC versions of QuickBooks Desktop. This is accounting software focused on small businesses for those who use a PC.

28

Where Does It Live?

The file can live on your desktop, on a server, or in the cloud. The cloud storage has an additional cost associated with it.

What Features Are Included?

All the basic features you would expect from accounting software are included. You can enter customers, vendors, perform journal entries, reconciliations, and so on.

What Features Are Forgotten?

The main features missing in QuickBooks Pro are the ability perform business specific reports, create and manage budgets, track 1099 contractors and access historical reconciliations. Additionally, the inventory features are not as advanced as the higher versions of QuickBooks and could be challenging if you have a complex product that you resell.

What's It Cost?

QuickBooks Pro costs an initial fee of $299. The annual subscription runs the same price. Hosting through QuickBooks also has additional costs associated with it.

Is It User-Friendly?

Desktop versions of QuickBooks are moderately user-friendly. Out of the box, there are a vast number of decisions the designated administrator must make, and initially this can be overwhelming. However, there are a handful of PC keyboard tricks that make it very user-friendly for PC addicts.

What Else Do You Need to Know About This Software?

The QuickBooks Pro software is really designed for a small business owner who prefers desktop software and is just starting out. The Pro version is great for one stream of revenue, a few bills, and a small list of expenses. It is also great as you grow your staff and add complexity to your accounting.

Final Thoughts

Overall, QuickBooks Pro is solid software focused on your current and future small business needs. It's a cost-effective solution for a very small team with fewer than three users and no need for creating and emailing sales orders. Initially the software is a bit overwhelming, but this book makes it less intimidating.

QuickBooks Premier

Who's It For?

QuickBooks Premier is a more advanced version of QuickBooks Desktop. This is accounting software focused on small businesses that are growing and have expanding needs. Additionally, this is for users who prefer to use PC-based software.

Where Does It Live?

The file can live on your desktop, on a server, or in the cloud. The cloud storage has an additional cost associated with it.

What Features Are Included?

All the basic features you would expect from accounting software are included, plus much more. You can enter customers, vendors, perform journal entries, reconciliations, and so on. Additionally, QuickBooks Premier offers 50+ additional reporting options above QuickBooks Pro as well as the ability to create build of materials (BOMs) and manufacture goods within the inventory center. You also have the ability to have up to five users work simultaneously.

What Features Are Forgotten?

QuickBooks Premier is very robust and covers most of the features needed to successfully account for your small business. The items that are forgotten are complex reporting and tracking features for small businesses that are scaling—these solutions can only be found in QuickBooks Enterprise.

What's It Cost?

QuickBooks Premier is $499 for a one-time software fee. The annual subscription is required and runs the same price every year after that. Hosting through QuickBooks also has additional costs associated with it.

Is It User-Friendly?

Desktop versions of QuickBooks are moderately user-friendly. Out of the box, there are a vast number of decisions the designated administrator must make, and initially this can be overwhelming. However, there are a handful of PC keyboard tricks that make it very user-friendly for PC addicts.

What Else Do You Need to Know About This Software?

QuickBooks Premier is really designed for a small business owner who prefers desktop software and is past the basic phase of their business. Premier is great for multiple streams of revenue, many bills, and any number of expenses. It is also robust and designed for an accounting team of five.

Final Thoughts

Overall, QuickBooks Premier is solid software focused on the needs of your growing small business now and in the future. It's a cost-effective solution that is great for smaller teams of up to five users. Initially the software is a bit overwhelming, but this book makes it less so.

QuickBooks Enterprise

Who's It For?

QuickBooks Enterprise is the most advanced version of QuickBooks on the market. This product's core consumer is a complex small to mid-size business with multiple individuals in the accounting department.

Where Does It Live?

This product could live on your corporate server or in the Intuit cloud.

What Features Are Included?

All the basic QuickBooks features are included and much more. Ever think you would like to track 1 million customers? Need 30 staff members working in QuickBooks at once? Need consolidated financial reports? QuickBooks Enterprise does all those things and has features built in to do even more.

What Features Are Forgotten?

In terms of QuickBooks, no features are forgotten. However, if you are considering QuickBooks Enterprise, you need to take a deep look at your firm's needs. QuickBooks Enterprise is robust software, but it is not nearly as robust as the financial enterprise resource planning (ERP) software on the market.

What's It Cost?

Depending on if hosting is included and how many users need access, the product price can range from $150 to $1,000 per month. Yes, we are talking about real robust accounting needs, and the price reflects that.

34

Is It User-Friendly?

The more basic features of QuickBooks Enterprise are similar to that of other QuickBooks products. They are easy to use and easy to learn. The more complex features of Enterprise can be challenging and take some time to learn for an untrained accountant.

What Else Do You Need to Know about This Software?

QuickBooks Enterprise is a robust software and the most advanced version of Intuit's QuickBooks product lines. This software is for expanding businesses that are outgrowing all the other basic products and need to manage lots of data or need to report on multiple entities. This is the most advanced QuickBooks software before transitioning to a truly custom accounting software such as an ERP.

A Quick Aside

For those of you who operate or plan on operating different entities (for example, you have an LLC for your digital products, an LLC for your brick and mortar retail, an S Corp for your management firm, etc.), you will need to understand the costs associated with choosing a version of QuickBooks software. The online version of QuickBooks charges you on a per-entity basis. So the key takeaway is that if you plan to manage multiple legal entities with QuickBooks, you really should look long and hard at the versions of QuickBooks Desktop before taking the leap with QuickBooks Online.

Chapter 5

Charting Your Accounts, AKA the Chart of Accounts

What Is a Chart of Accounts?

Merriam-Webster defines a chart of accounts as a list of account names arranged systematically and usually coded numerically or alphabetically or both to form the general framework of the accounting system of a specific business and to establish a scheme of account classification.

In layman's terms, the chart of accounts is a list of expenses or incomes that have numbers associated with them. These items are used to prepare financial statements. It really is that simple: a chart of accounts is a list of items used to help you prepare better financial statements. There is some method behind the madness of the crazy numbering, subaccounts, and other complexities. But the chart of accounts in QuickBooks is simply a framework to make accounting easier.

Why Is Accounting like Building a Home?

To first understand the need for a chart of accounts in QuickBooks, you must first understand how a home is constructed. A house begins as a thought. This mental process often begins before construction or land purchase. It starts off as a family's desire to have a place where they can share their memories. Your business begins the same way. It's an idea, a thought—one that could transform your life and give you the freedom to make your own path.

The next step in the process, once you get serious about building a home, is acquiring the land necessary to build the home. In the world of business ownership and accounting, QuickBooks is like the land the house is built on. It is where the business will be built—where the chart of accounts will be set up. If the land is where your home lives, then you can think of QuickBooks as the place where your business information lives. Just as land turns the idea of a home into a reality, your purchase of QuickBooks turns your business ideas into success.

The next step in homebuilding is often reaching out to an architect and developing plans. This equates to developing the chart of accounts. To better set up QuickBooks, you will use the chart of accounts provided below and modify it for your particular needs. This would be like buying a home in a neighborhood where the developer has a few different home models, and the end customer can modify the home finishes.

Once the home is built to specification, or once you have set up QuickBooks and the chart of accounts, including bank accounts, importing first expenses, and billing clients/entering sales, it is ready to "inhabit." The early tasks may initially seem tedious, but working through them ensures your business is in as tidy an order as a house that has been carefully and efficiently unpacked.

Running your business is like living in your home. Like a home, a business needs constant upkeep and cleaning. It also needs maintenance. QuickBooks and your chart of accounts can help you keep up. Additionally, QuickBooks may expand or contract. You may add a room to your house, and similarly in business, you add new accounts. You may realize that you no longer need an extra bedroom and just use it for storage, perhaps even downsizing your home or, comparably, removing items from your chart of accounts.

Why Are the Chart of Accounts So Important?

Oftentimes we hear people harp on the importance of one item or another: You must do this or do that to be successful. A majority of you have heard this and followed your own path, but the chart of accounts is truly important, so don't skim the next few pages.

The reality of a good chart of accounts is that it makes your life easier in both a business analysis and a tax reporting context. Let's say you run a complex retail business and have salespeople on the floor, management managing those people, production employees, and their managers. Yes, all of the above items are payroll expenses for your small firm, but business decisions cannot be made by looking at that number in total. The chart of accounts helps to break up this number. By breaking it up into departments and even roles (such as management versus nonmanagement), you will be able to see on a weekly, monthly, quarterly, and yearly basis how productive your team is, how much revenue was created by payroll expenses, and how much product was added to inventory by payroll expenses.

Let's take this example a step further. By focusing on the week-over-week expense for these departments and roles, you should be able to establish a minimum operating expense and, respectively, a quality operating percentage for when the business gets busy. More salespeople are obviously necessary as business picks up, but it may be more valuable to make some customers wait five minutes than lose money on a given day. By extrapolating those numbers with an in-depth chart of accounts from which you can run actual reports, you will be able to make better business decisions.

A well-established chart of accounts in QuickBooks helps you run your business better. How much are you spending on client meals? How much is your payroll costing you? How many refunds did you have last week? All these answers can be pulled from a quality chart of accounts, so pay attention!

Example of a Chart of Accounts

QuickBooks comes preloaded with a few different chart of account templates. You will be asked what industry you operate within, and then you will be given a preset chart of accounts. The offerings may have too few or too many accounts and subaccounts, or, on the other hand, it may have too few. So feel free to use the chart of accounts provided.

Below, I will give you in-depth insight into the QuickBooks Chart of Accounts, their categories, and the associated items with each category. This will lead you down the path of generating the best chart of accounts for your business. Let's be real, at the end of the day, the chart of accounts in QuickBooks is here to serve you.

What Is the Idea Behind the Chart of Accounts Structure?

The chart of accounts is designed to help you organize your business income and expenses. An extension of a chart of accounts is a profit and loss statement. A profit and loss statement (otherwise known as an income statement) shows the profitability of a business during a period of time. It is much more useful to a business operator when it does not break everything down into tiny little bits such as accounts, subaccounts, sub-sub-accounts. The most useful profit and loss statement fits onto just a page or two, so don't let this turn into a five-page report. If you want to get detailed information on certain accounts, that is what all the robust reporting features inside QuickBooks are built for.

How Do I Standardize My Chart of Accounts (and Make Sure I Make My CPA Happy)?

I hear it all the time: How do I standardize my chart of accounts or make the chart of account comply with Generally Accepted Accounting Principles? Below highlights some of the more standard procedures, but remember one of the major goals of accounting is to serve the business owner's needs—so make your chart of accounts work for you.

A standard chart of accounts is organized according to a numerical system. Remember when you learned to count to ten as a child? We are just going to relearn how to do that, but this time each number is going to mean something different.

Each major category begins with a certain number, and then the subcategories within that major category all begin with the same number. For example, if assets are classified by numbers starting with the digit 1, then cash accounts might be labeled 1001, accounts receivable might be labeled 1002, inventory might be labeled 1003, and so on. If liabilities accounts are classified by numbers starting with the digit 2, then accounts payable might be labeled 2001, short-term debt might be labeled 2002, and so on.

Depending on the size and complexity of your company, the chart of accounts may include a few dozen accounts or it may include a hundred (super complex businesses can have thousands).

Below is a quick cheat sheet to help you structure your chart of accounts.

1000 – 1999 Assets
2000 – 2999 Liabilities
3000 – 3999 Equity
4000 – 4999 Income or Revenue
5000 – 5999 Cost of Goods Sold

6000 – 6999 Expenses
7000 – 7999 Other Income
8000 – 8999 Other Expenses

What Do You Mean the Chart of Accounts Has Categories?

At this point you may be in information overload mode—overwhelmed. Don't fret, it is not as complicated as you think, especially in QuickBooks. You may have heard some of the terms above or not. We will dive into each one in a simple format to help you better understand them.

Assets: 1000 – 1999

Assets are items that your company owns. For example, you could own the money in your bank account or own the computer you are reading this book on. This is usually divided into two categories, and QuickBooks helps you divide it. These categories are current assets and fixed assets.

Current assets are items that can quickly be turned into cash, such as the money in your bank account. (Of course, even though you can put your car on Craigslist and quickly sell the clunker, it is not considered a current asset.) Some other items that may be current assets are savings accounts, money market accounts, accounts receivable, and inventory.

Fixed assets are items you would usually have to sell to generate cash. The minimum amount for fixed assets is often $500. Some examples of these items are that clunker mentioned above, machinery, equipment, computer, cars, and so on.

Liabilities: 2000 – 2999

Liabilities are the money your company owes other people. Did you borrow $1,000 from your buddy to cover payroll on that week sales were slow? Well that would be a liability for your entity. Do you collect sales tax that you need to remit to the government? That is a liability because you owe that money, and it is not yours.

Equity: 3000 – 3999

Equity accounts really depend on how your entity is structured, and they vary depending on if your entity is a sole proprietorship (single member LLC), partnership (multiple member LLC), or corporation.

In QuickBooks, if your entity is a sole proprietorship, you need a Capital account and an Owner's Draw account. The Capital account is to keep track of just that, the total capital (or amount of money) you have invested since starting the business, plus or minus the net profit or loss each year since you started the business. Use the Owner's Draw account for money you take out of the business for personal use, such as paying your car note or an Xbox for little Jimmy, cash withdrawals, your distributions, and any money that gets deposited into your personal accounts.

Pro Tip

Note that as a sole proprietor (single member LLC) you do not pay yourself as a regular employee via W-2. You need to distribute and pay taxes on that money. Consult with your CPA to ensure you are following the correct protocol.

If your company is a partnership (think multimember LLC) or Limited Liability Partnership (LLP), you need to set up Capital and Draw accounts for each partner in QuickBooks. For example, Uncle Todd gave you some money to start your business, and your wife's dad Joe also kicked in some cash. They would need QuickBooks accounts titled Uncle Todd's Capital and Uncle Todd's Draw. Similarly, Joe would need Wife's Dad Joe Capital and Wife's Dad Joe Draw. As an aside, the money contributed to open the business goes into the Capital account and the money distributed is coded to Draw.

If your company is an S or C corporation or an LLC corporation (different from an LLC partnership), it should have a Common Stock account and sometimes a Preferred Stock account. Common Stock and Preferred Stock represent the total sum of stock the company has issued. An LLC might have member stock if there is more than one person who owns stock. This is a bit more on the complex level, and you should refer to your CPA to ensure you set up these accounts correctly based on your entity type and member structure.

Income or Revenue: 4000 – 4999

Income or revenue is the income your business gets from day-to-day business operations. These include, but are not limited to, consulting fees, income for services rendered, reimbursable expenses, or products you sell. Structuring these accounts in QuickBooks is really up to you. Perhaps you run two different departments for your business, then you may want to separate them into subaccounts of income. Or maybe you sell multiple types of products in each department, then you may want sub-sub-accounts. Either way, it's best to remember that less is more.

Oftentimes, refunds and exchanges live in this category. This ensures that your net profit is truly your net profit. Your top line revenue number should be the money you received for the period, not the money received before refunds and item comps.

Cost of Goods Sold (A.K.A. COGS): 5000 – 5999

In QuickBooks, the Cost of Goods Sold includes the cost of raw materials, freight charges for getting raw material to a warehouse, labor for building the finished goods, and freight charges for getting the goods to the customer. For manufacturing businesses, the Cost of Goods Sold includes the costs incurred in producing or building a product. For a wholesale business, Cost of Goods Sold includes the costs of the goods you purchase for resale. For a distributor business, Cost of Goods Sold includes the costs to purchase and distribute goods to the customer. These costs tend to increase as you sell more products or services. If you sold no goods or services, this account should not incur any expenses.

Let's look at the restaurant business as an example. The restaurant's main inputs are the food bought to produce the dishes on the menu. Some operators prefer to see one lump sum of purchases while other choose to break it out into their main inputs of meat, dairy, baked goods, and dry goods. Be creative, figure out what will make your business function better, set guidelines, and follow them.

Expenses: 6000 – 6999

Expenses are the fixed costs that exist even if you sell no products or services. Examples include rent, telephone, insurance, vehicle expense, advertising, and utilities.

Other Income: 7000 – 7999

Other Income in QuickBooks is income you earn outside the normal way you do business, including interest income, gain on the sale of an asset, insurance settlement, a stock sale, or rents from buildings you own when real estate is not your main business focus.

It is likely that you will not use this income type very often.

Other Expenses: 8000 – 8999

Other Expenses refer to an expense that is outside of your normal business, such as a loss on the sale of an asset, or stockbroker fees (though it is not limited to these items and also often includes depreciation, amortization, R&D expenses, finance cost, and income tax expenses).

What is the General Ledger?

For all general purposes, the chart of accounts in QuickBooks is very similar to the general ledger. To be more precise, the general ledger is the numbered accounts based off the chart of accounts and stores all the financial transactions for the life of your firm. A general ledger account is an account or record used to sort and store balance sheet and income statement transactions. Examples of general ledger accounts include everything from cash and bank accounts to salary expense and revenue.

Let's say you wanted to see what has gone on in your firm over the past six months. Well, obviously you sit in the office or garage if you are the next Apple and see what is going on in your business. More importantly, you want to see what your company is spending your hard-earned money on, so you use QuickBooks to run the General Ledger report.

This report shows all the transactions that took place within your business and to what codes these items were classified. It really paints a picture of what is going on in your firm, answering questions such as, *why are my advertising expenses so high for the year?* and, *what is going on with my payroll?* Running the General Ledger report for a large period lets you see the fluctuations of certain expenses over a period. For example, has your weekly payroll run doubled? Did the new staff result in a hit in profitability? Did your daily sales revenue decline in the summer time?

Taking a look at your general ledger lets you get very granular about your business and what is going on within it. Reviewing this report also ensures that your staff or you have been recording transactions properly. Are all your credit card fees in the right place? Or, do you have all your payroll in the "Legal and Professional Fees" category and legal and professional fees in the "Payroll Expense" category?

> Pro Tip
>
> Make sure your general ledger is in order now! This makes the closing of the year and preparing of your tax returns a breeze come March. Remember, plan for success, or don't plan and fail.

What Does a Sample Chart of Accounts Look Like?

Account #	Account Name	Type
1010	Checking Account	Bank
1020	Savings Account	Bank
1030	Cash on Hand	Bank
1100	Accounts Receivable	Accounts Receivable
1200	Inventory Asset	Other Current Asset
1400	Prepaid Expenses	Other Current Asset
1410	Processor 1 Receivable	Other Current Asset
1420	Processor 2 Receivable	Other Current Asset
1430	Processor 3 Receivable	Other Current Asset
1440	Employee Cash Advances	Other Current Asset
1500	Furniture and Fixtures	Fixed Asset

1510	Machinery and Equipment	Fixed Asset
1520	Vehicles	Fixed Asset
1530	Other Fixed Assets	Fixed Asset
1540	Leasehold Improvements	Fixed Asset
1599	Accumulated Depreciation	Fixed Asset
1900	Security Deposit Asset	Other Asset
1910	Organizational Cost	Other Asset
1920	Accumulated Amortization	Other Asset
2000	Accounts Payable	Accounts Payable
2100	Salaries Payable	Other Current Liabilities
2200	Sales Tax Payable	Other Current Liabilities
2300	Federal Income Tax Payable	Other Current Liabilities
2400	Unearned Revenue	Other Current Liabilities
2500	Notes Payable	Other Current Liabilities
2600	Bank Loan	Long Term Liabilities
3000	Opening Balance Equity	Equity
3100	Partner 1 Contributions	Equity
3200	Partner 1 Distributions	Equity
3300	Partner 1 Contributions	Equity
3400	Partner 2 Distributions	Equity

4100	Sale of Product Income	Income
4200	Refunds	Income
4300	Discounts	Income
4400	Other Primary Income	Income
5100	Cost of Goods Sold	Cost of Goods Sold
5200	Supplies and Materials	Cost of Goods Sold
5300	Change in Inventory	Cost of Goods Sold
6000	Payroll	Expense
6010	Payroll Wages (Sub)	Expense
6020	Payroll Taxes (Sub)	Expense
6030	Employee Benefits (Sub)	Expense
6040	Payroll Processing Fee (Sub)	Expense
6100	Advertising and Promotion	Expense
6150	Marketing	Expense
6200	Bank Fees	Expense
6210	Bank Fees (Sub)	Expense
6220	Credit Card Fees (Sub)	Expense
6300	General and Administrative	Expense
6310	Dues and Subscriptions (Sub)	Expense
6320	Office Supplies (Sub)	Expense

6330	Office Equipment (Sub)	Expense
6340	Postage (Sub)	Expense
6400	Research and Development	Expense
6500	Insurance Expense	Expense
6550	Interest Expense	Expense
6600	Legal & Professional Fees	Expense
6610	Accounting Fees (Sub)	Expense
6620	Legal Fees (Sub)	Expense
6630	Professional Fees (Sub)	Expense
6650	License Expense	Expense
6700	Meals and Entertainment	Expense
6710	Automobile Expense	Expense
6720	Travel expense	Expense
6800	Facilities	Expense
6810	Rent or Lease Expense (Sub)	Expense
6820	Utilities (Sub)	Expense
6830	Telephone and Internet (Sub)	Expense
6840	Repair and Maintenance (Sub)	Expense
6900	Penalties and Fines	Expense
6990	Ask My Accountant	Expense

8100	Tax Expense	Other Expense
8200	Bad Debt	Other Expense
8300	Amortization Expense	Other Expense
8400	Depreciation Expense	Other Expense
9000	Gain on Sales of Asset	Other Income

Pro Tip

The above chart of accounts is merely a guide. You need to make adjustments to fit your business and industry. For example, do you have multiple payroll departments? Break them out in subcategories under Salaries and Wages. Do you have multiple profit centers? Break them out in the 4000s. Do you pay rent on both a warehouse and office space? Create subcategories for these items so you can see which expense created which revenue. Are you spending too much on shipping and warehousing? The chart of account should help you figure this out.

Chapter 6

Automate Your Accounting World

How to Make Technology Work for You

Earlier we learned the benefits of fantastic software that does not require double entries for every one transaction. The benefits of technology do not stop there. With the advent of computer apps like QBO, many companies have generated software that allows apps to communicate with each other.

The below is a simplified example of the conversation your apps can have with each other. Of course, this communication takes place in code and happens instantaneously.

Internet Point of Sale: Hi, QuickBooks Online, yesterday, Monday, March 21st, 2018, we sold $595 on your website.

QuickBooks Online: Okay great, we will add these sales to the system; can you give me details on the transactions?

Internet Point of Sale: Sure, $495 was from credit cards and $100 was from PayPal.

Automation can come in many forms. The overall idea is to make the accounting easier so that it requires fewer man hours. There are many platforms and software programs that can help you with this process. For those not using QBO there are also other ways to import sales or automate your sales that require some work on your behalf but that save hours of manual entry.

Automate Today, Tomorrow, and Next Month

Technology is often seen as a challenge, similar to the way one sees QuickBooks when logging in for the first time. As stated earlier, QuickBooks is a tool to accomplish your goals, and so is technology as a whole.

The benefits of automation run deep. For a small business with annual sales of roughly $1 million USD, it could require up to one business day a week to enter all the sales data necessary to keep sales up to date. The annual cost of this part-time data entry position could easily exceed $10,000. The costs can add up quickly.

When you begin to automate parts of your accounting world, the world of financial reporting becomes easier. The complex sales data you need is already available and in the correct formats. The general ledger accounts are debited and credited correctly. The reports based on certain period dates are correct. The decisions you make based upon your business are correct. All of these equate to your business being on track.

Applications and QuickBooks

There are plenty of apps options currently on the market to help you automate your accounting. We will look at the some of the top players currently in the space and the import/export feature that will never be outdated.

App Connectors

Some of the most popular technology right now is in the form of services that connect multiple apps. For example, your Instagram can talk to an Excel file or your CRM can talk to QuickBooks.

Personally, I have had a lot of success with software that serves as connector. It tracks communication clearly, notifies you of any issues, and—most importantly—keeps accurate data.

In terms of QuickBooks, the ability to pull data from multiple sources is a blessing. You could pull information from your CRM to your payment processors. If you can use the features, do it—but make sure you set them up properly!

Exporting from Your Point of Sale

Many older points of sale (POS) offer a feature where you can export the data to both QuickBooks Desktop and QBO. If you properly close out your days in your

POS, denoting cash over or short, which checks have been deposited, and which credit cards have been processed, all this data can be imported to save the time of manual entry. This simple file import is a true blessing.

Oftentimes this feature is covered in the onboarding process with your POS. This is considered a classic feature where you would import an IIF or an XML file. Having been around for quite some time, this approach has been perfected.

Having used features like this at large organizations, I have found it beneficial in terms of time savings and accuracy. Adjustments can be made after the fact. The data is imported in a simple fashion and the after-the-fact adjustments can simply be made on the daily entry where it is needed.

Overall, you should really consider how your POS will interact with your accounting software as part of your search for the right solution. Not only does it need to interface well with your staff and the customer, but you need it to serve as a financial tool for you. If you can't get accurate reports or data, how will your business ever succeed?

Auto-Importing Features

Lots of points of sale offer QBO integration features. Initially these seem like a great option for automating your business and saving money. Of course that's the goal, but it must be done correctly. Let's dive in a bit further.

When dealing with complex daily sales and revenue that is deposited through multiple transaction types (credit card processors, revenue centers), you need proper tracking to reconcile your books correctly. An example of multiple transaction types for credit card processors would be the following: Visa, MasterCard, Amex, cash, and gift card. These transaction types should be deposited into different clearing accounts within your balance sheet. By putting them in separate clearing accounts, you can simultaneously reconcile accounts to ensure all your money is there. The challenge with many of the points of sale that automate this process is that they offer one limited solution for all your transactions.

For example, some points of sale will essentially create a pretend bank and deposit all your invoices into that account. These deposits do not actually occur so they will not match actual bank deposits, and oftentimes there are refunds or processing fees that need to be added after the fact. This is one hundred percent the incorrect way to process these transactions. There are two reasons why: One, the deposit has not been differentiated based on processor or transaction type. Two, all that data is really not necessary for QuickBooks. If you have it in your POS and have recorded the records, you are fine.

To ensure you are booking sales properly, you need to understand how the POS is importing data. If it splits the data by revenue and transaction types in a nice journal entry, then this is correct. If it brings in each individual invoice and does not allow for you to break out by revenue type and transaction type with nowhere to book your credit card fees, then stay away!

The main difference between this and the auto-importing I will discuss shortly is that exporting from your POS will bring in the total amounts for the day as opposed to individual sales receipts or invoices. This makes dealing with your books much easier and managing the sales if there is a reconciliation issue a breeze.

Overall Thoughts on Automation

Automation at its core is fantastic, it saves time and makes your life simpler. Unfortunately, not all the apps or POS features in the market function at the level necessary for your accounting success. In other words, all integrations are not created equal.

Take your time and research your options. You may even want to perform a small sales test prior to committing to a full-on integration. See if setting up the data to automatically import works for your case. If not, then you may just be stuck doing the sales entries by hand for some time. Don't fret though, you are not alone in that!

QBO App Store

The QBO App Store is a great place and the home of many integrations to save you time and money. Ever wanted to import the customer information from your CRM into QuickBooks to better invoice clients? You can do that. Ever wanted to import employee time tracking to better pay employees on a weekly basis? You can do that. It does not stop there, plenty of integrations exist.

The key to setting up a good integration is to read the reviews. See how other users are experiencing these apps. Like any app marketplace there are good and bad eggs. See how the product is working for other people in your space, and remember that you can always try the data on a single day or a single batch of information. Thus, in a worst-case scenario, you can easily delete the information to undo what you incorrectly imported.

Chapter 7

Set A Weekly Schedule

Why Get Organized?

Organization for some comes with ease. For others, it's a daunting nightmare. Are you the former or the latter? If you are the former, skim the following pages. If you are the latter, read three times.

Running a business is very similar to running a household. If you do not set aside the time throughout the year to clean or do not bring in someone else to clean, your home will be disgusting by the end of the year. If you do not have a family calendar on the fridge or on everyone's smartphone, appointments and practices will surely be missed. If you are like me, you create a schedule and set aside time every fourth weekend to do a deep cleaning, and every other weekend do a light cleaning. If you are like me, you have a calendar shared on your smartphone and an itemized shopping list shared in a sharing software. It is very likely that you are not like me yet, and that is why I will give you the tools you need to get organized.

In the world of accounting, lack of structure means lack of organization, which results in missing important dates and deadlines, often with very serious ramifications. What would your employees do if you missed their direct deposit deadline week after week? They would go work for someone else! No matter how understanding and caring a leader you are, if you don't stay organized, you are burning your organization down from the inside.

Why Weekly?

Choosing a weekly structure is not a lucky guess or some crazy idea pulled from the sky. To make conscious and accurate business decisions, you need data on a regular and routine basis. Accounting on a weekly basis allows you to look at the minor details of your organization and catch oddities before they become nuclear disasters.

Most small and new businesses live and breathe by cash flow. They often pay employees on a weekly basis to properly manage this cash flow. By looking at sales over cost of goods sold and expenses (such as payroll), you can quickly map a structure through which to learn in-depth about your business.

A weekly structure also makes sense for a less profound reason—we think in days. We plan our weeks around which night we will cook in or go out to eat. We plan our weeks around which days the kids are going to what practice. We plan our life around weeks. Thinking in terms of business, if someone said to do cash deposits on the third Tuesday of the month, why wait to put cash into the bank for almost 30 days? That is asking for a disaster situation and an inability to pay the bills.

Now if I said you need to deposit cash weekly, the wheels in your head start turning. You may say to yourself, *well, my daughter's softball practice is*

Thursday evening at 6—the bank is on the way, why not stop then? Now instead of creating a complex schedule that makes your life more challenging, you've created a schedule that fits into your realm of routines. Perhaps you do not have kids but you always have lunch around the same shopping area on Saturday. I guarantee that you will find one bank open on Saturday, or your banks will allow for an overnight deposit. Either way, you can deposit the cash on the way to your favorite lunch spot without worrying about compromising your life or not accomplishing the task on a weekly basis.

Here Is an Example

Years ago I ran an organization with a hundred employees and a few million dollars in revenue. We did not have a complex accounting staff or much above the level of QuickBooks Pro in our toolkit. What led us down the road to success, you may ask? A clear and concise weekly schedule that ensured all deposits were made and reporting correct.

Here is a version of that schedule:

Monday
- Check mail, record all deposits and invoices received.
- Record sales from previous week (Tuesday until Sunday).
- Update online banking (Tuesday until Friday).*

Tuesday
- Make cash and check deposits.
- Finish online banking (for Monday).
- Cut checks for the week (mailing out Tuesday will ensure receipt by Friday).

Wednesday
- Review weekly profit and loss statement.
- Hold all staff meetings associated with finance.

Thursday
- Check mail again, record all invoices received.
- Perform weekly payroll run.

Friday
- Resolve any other outstanding items (re-class expenses, follow up on payments, fix any incorrect checks, etc.).

*Saturday and Sunday banking usually do not clear until Tuesday morning.

The above business reflects a retail business, so a certain importance is placed on specific items. Some of the tasks would differ depending on the field your business operates within. For example, those in consulting or services need to invoice clients on a weekly or monthly basis. Scheduling invoices would need to be added to your schedule to ensure that you invoice quickly and receive prompt payment.

What's the Logic?

The above schedule is a great starter for any small business. The key is not as much which days certain items are completed but rather why they were done on those days. Are you updating your banking for a meeting? Are you mailing checks out so they reach your vendor by the end of the week? Tailor the schedule to work for you and your business, just make sure you understand the logic behind it.

The overall goal is to have accurate and true financials. What's the point of holding a weekly staff meeting and discussing your numbers if the numbers are not accurate? If you are discussing the previous week and none of the invoices are in, you are not tracking the expenses of the firm. If your firm has multiple departments, and you are meeting with a department head, but you have not reviewed the expense he is responsible for—what was the point of the meeting? Having the tools you and your staff need to succeed are crucial to the overall success of the company!

When running a small business, you live and die by your numbers. These figures decide if you can make the much needed new hire or reinvest in your infrastructure. If your numbers are not updated on a weekly basis so you can take a look at weekly financials, then what is the point of the numbers?

As a business owner, you will often have a long-term plan and a short-term plan. These plans will likely have monetary goals attached to them. By setting budget, expenses, or other operating margins against these timelines, you can see if you are succeeding or failing. Don't walk into your meetings empty handed. Ensure you follow a weekly routine so your numbers are prepared and ready to help you make the best possible decision, because at the end of the day that is your job as the business owner.

Chapter 8

Reconcile Your Domicile

What Is Reconciling?

In layman's terms, reconciling means providing verification that an account balance is correct. For example, we reconcile the balance in the checking account to the balance shown on the bank statement. The objective is to report the correct amount in your checking account in QuickBooks. By reconciling this account you will ensure that you did not miss that crazy bank fee or the receipt from the gas station one employee forgot to turn in.

The Generally Accepted Accounting Principles (GAAP) are a set of accounting principles, procedures, and standards that organizations use in order to compile their financial statements. Generally Accepted Accounting Principles states that the purpose of account reconciliation is to provide accuracy and consistency in financial accounts. To ensure all cash outlays and inlays match between cash flow statements and income statements, it is necessary to carry out reconciliation accounts.

Reconciliation is a process that will benefit your business because it helps avoid errors that may lead to detrimental ramifications. Do you really want to give your business partner a report showing you made money when you didn't? In the world of business, your word is everything. If your financials are based on your word, but those financials are incorrect, well, unfortunately, your word is incorrect. Reconciliation also plays a valuable role in helping against fraud and ensuring financial integrity.

Additionally, reconciliations help you spot checks that haven't cleared from months before. Is this vendor still owed money? Was it a duplicated transaction? If so, it needs to be removed, and your financial statements need to be redone. Ultimately, reconciling helps spot errors and ensure you fix them in a timely fashion.

Why Worry About This Reconciling Thing?

Reconciling your books is like taking a test in school. Everyone hates it no matter how good of a student they are. Tests are designed to determine if you mastered the materials that have been studied in the previous period. Like tests, reconciling analyzes your QuickBooks entries to ensure the previous period represents a true and accurate financial picture. We will get into the intricate details of reconciling in this chapter, but more importantly, you need to understand the importance of reconciling.

As you become more experienced within QuickBooks, you may come to find making sales entries and paying bills is a fun and exciting activity. You will use this information to make business decisions and move your enterprise forward. How does one ensure that the information on hand is correct? That is where reconciling comes in—it ensures that all the transactions in your reports are correct and true to form.

Reconciling helps you spot inconsistencies in your books. Perhaps you worked all week and then came home and made some late night transactions in QuickBooks on Friday evening. At the end of the month you will reconcile these transactions and catch that late-night mistake you made! Reconciling ensures that errors don't go on for months and years but are resolved within a few weeks.

Additionally, reconciling plays a key role in ensuring that all your money is where it is supposed to be. For example, perhaps you take credit card payments on your tablet or deposit cash weekly at the bank. Oftentimes your credit card processor forgets to batch your money, and sometimes your bank forgets to apply deposits to your account. Crazy as it might sound, it happens all the time—to the tune of hundreds of thousands of dollars. I have seen it firsthand—reconciling ensures that those errors are caught well before you need the money.

Before You Reconcile

Before you reconcile your accounts, check these things:

Be sure you're up to date on entering your transactions in QuickBooks. You know that check you wrote last week for your rent but didn't enter in QuickBooks, or the bills you paid but haven't marked them as paid in QuickBooks? Do that now. Enter all transactions that haven't cleared or shown up on previous bank statements.

The very first time you reconcile, check the Opening Balance transaction on your bank accounts in your QuickBooks Chart of Accounts. They should reflect the amount that was actually in your account when you began using QuickBooks. If it doesn't match, you can fix this by following the below steps:

In your QuickBooks Chart of Accounts, open the register for the account (double-click the account name) and change the Opening Balance transaction to match the ending balance from the last bank statement you received before you started using QuickBooks. The Opening Balance is usually the first transaction that appears within the register.

More importantly, you must have all your ducks in a row. Have your statements printed, a coffee, your pen, and a comfy chair. The first time you do this will be challenging, but I promise it gets easier from here.

How Do I Reconcile?

QuickBooks Online

QuickBooks Online makes reconciliations a breeze. First, you must navigate to the Reconcile menu. To do this, simply start at the home screen, click on the Gear menu, and beneath the column heading Tools, select the Reconcile tab.

The next step is probably your most important—which account will you reconcile? It is important to reconcile all the accounts that I highlight in this chapter. Depending on how your business is set up, it is most beneficial to reconcile receivables, cash on hand, and credit cards prior to your bank account. This helps ensure you track complex errors before doing your bank reconciliation, so you do not have to redo it. Choose the account you want to reconcile from the drop-down menu options (all the accounts are explained below). Once you've selected your account, click Reconcile Now.

Now you must enter your statement details. For bank statements, you just need to enter the end date and ending amount. For items like receivables, cash on hand, etc. you can enter $0 or the actual ending amount. Let's say you have $400 in the cash register draw, that should be your beginning or ending balance. You could also pretend like the $400 does not exist and count based off of $0 for the beginning and ending.

Now the real work begins. Take another look at the transaction history on your bank statement. In the Reconcile window, match each transaction from your bank statement with an item in the list, checking the box to the right of each transaction to match. If you are reconciling other accounts like receivables, just ensure that your outflows match your inflows. For example, if you booked $1,000 in sales on the 5th, you should see that deposit on the 8th.

Now you can finish your reconciliation. When you've gotten the difference value at the bottom to zero you are all set. Though it is important to understand that you don't just want a zero ending balance, but rather you want all your transactions that are checked to match those on your statement with a zero ending balance. Clearing transactions for next month while working on last month's bank statements makes no sense!

QuickBooks Desktop (all versions)

QuickBooks Desktop makes reconciliation a bit more challenging, or just more unfriendly to the eyes. To begin your reconciliation, visit the Banking menu and select Reconcile (this option also exists on the home screen, that thing that pops up every time you start QuickBooks).

You will then be prompted to select which account you would like to reconcile, as we discussed above. As indicated above, you enter your account's ending balance in the ending balance section along with the ending date. Then you click continue to begin the reconciliation.

Then check items as they appear on your bank account statement. As you work down the bank statement, your different amount should approach zero, and when your difference is zero and all the monthly items listed on your bank statement are included, congrats! You can click Reconcile Now, and the reconciliation is complete.

What Exactly Should I Reconcile?

Below is a list of all the accounts you should reconcile and a short background on why they are important.

Bank Account

As you are beginning to realize, reconciling is of the utmost importance. There are multiple accounts that should be reconciled on a monthly basis to ensure accuracy of your accounting—most importantly, the bank account.

Small businesses live and breathe by cash flow or cash on hand. If no cash is on hand, no bills can be paid. If no bills can be paid, employees can't be paid, new inventory can't be bought, the website shuts down, and so on.

QuickBooks gives you an account balance in the bank account based on the transactions within QuickBooks. When you cut checks, hopefully you cut checks so that the balance does not fall below zero. If you have payroll or a tax liability due in the near future, you need to ensure that the checks you cut now and the future payables combined do not fall below the dreaded zero mark. Reconciling your bank account ensures that the numbers you base your decisions on are actually accurate.

Some of you may have multiple bank accounts. For example, you could have a payroll clearing account, a sales tax liability account, multiple checking accounts for various locations, and so on. Reconciling all bank accounts where money is held should be your number one priority on a monthly basis.

Reconciling your bank accounts also serves an additional purchase rarely mentioned. Reconciling these accounts on a regular basis ensures you are protected from fraud. Fraud of all types occurs in the world of business. Perhaps someone got ahold of a check or your debit card. By reconciling your account on a regular basis you protect yourself from having these transactions go unnoticed. By being aware of these occurrences, you can react in a timely fashion by canceling cards or transferring to a new account with new bank account numbers.

Liabilities

Liabilities, liabilities, liabilities: They are the root of small business failure. Leverage and debt are great for growing your small business as they allow you to use less of your own capital to get outsized returns. These liabilities are often due on a monthly basis, and this means the outstanding balance must be correct before your payment is due.

Credit Cards

Oftentimes, small businesses will give all their employees credit cards because these employees wear many hats—often running to the post office, entertaining a client, making an online purchase, etc. It is vital to ensure that each credit card is reconciled and that there are no nasty surprises hidden away. You want to know in advance if an employee went Christmas shopping on your card!

As mentioned previously, fraud is a major issue when it comes to credit cards, so by ensuring the credit card balances are correct, you ensure that your business metrics are correct. By reconciling your account, you are positive that the charges are correct, and when any surprises arise, you can find out the root of the charge.

Receivables

Perhaps you accept credit cards for your business, or maybe you have a payment processor that deposits every few days. This is considered a receivable, and you want to ensure that you receive all the money that is rightfully yours when you are supposed to.

Booking accurate sales in your system is very important but only half the battle. More important than booking the correct sale is ensuring you get your money. A simple receivable reconciliation can be performed on a weekly or monthly basis.

Oftentimes credit card processors or POS systems hold back money or don't deposit the correct amount. It is your job as the business owner to ensure all the right amounts are deposited. I have occasionally seen processors simply forget to make deposits or hold back money for some wild reason that takes faxing over paperwork to resolve. Either way, by reconciling your receivables you can ensure that you are getting all the money that is rightfully yours.

Payables

Like the many other accounts that need to be reconciled, you must ensure that your payables number matches that of your payables on your balance sheet. This can be a bit confusing at first, but overall you want the bills you have to pay to be showing up properly in your accounts payable.

Before closing the books at the end of each reporting period, you must verify that the detailed total of all accounts payable outstanding matches the payables account balance stated in the general ledger. Doing so ensures that the amount of accounts payable reported in the balance sheet is correct. This is called an accounts payable reconciliation.

This reconciliation process can be a difficult one when performed for the first time. However, once all errors have been spotted and corrections made, it is usually relatively easy to update the reconciliation document in subsequent reporting periods.

Cash on Hand

The hard cash that you have in your possession or sitting around the office is very important and is referred to as petty cash or cash on hand. You oftentimes pay small bills out of this, or large ones if you frequently deal in cash. These are all business expenses, and it is your job to track these transactions. That is where reconciling cash on hand comes in, allowing you to ensure that all your cash expenditures are accounted for.

Let's say you start the period with $500 in cash on hand locked away in your safe. At the end of the

84

month you count the safe and only have $405 left. It is recommended that you have a place for your receipts or trade receipts for dollars throughout the month. Either way, you should count up those receipts and ensure they match the missing $95. QuickBooks allows you to track all those transactions, and you should. All the receipts should be entered and the cash on hand bank used as the method of purchase.

Now what if you don't have all the receipts of your missing $95 This is a prime example as to why you reconcile often and ensure everything is accounted for. Perhaps your employee ran to the store to get office supplies and forgot to give you the receipt. Or worst-case scenario, perhaps someone in the office has sticky fingers—you need to figure out who it is and how handle it, because $95 an quickly turn into $500.

Fixing Broken Reconciliations

There will be times when you will have worked diligently to update your QuickBooks—adding all the transactions, writing checks out of the system, matching everything to the correct general ledger code—but can't seem to make your reconciliations work.

Well, here are a few potential reasons your reconciliations are broken:

1. You changed something in a previous period that affects a current reconciliation.
2. You are missing transactions from a current reconciliation that needs to be added in.
3. You entered transactions or wrote checks from the wrong account in QuickBooks.

To Resolve a Previous Period Issue

Compare the ending account balance in the general ledger for the immediately preceding period to the starting amount in your reconciliation window. Do they match? If these numbers do not match, you will have to reconcile earlier periods before attempting to reconcile the current period.

QuickBooks has a feature called "Locate Discrepancies." This should help you find the transaction that was changed, deleted, or added. Take a look at the report and see if the transactions remind you of a previous transaction that exists, does not exist, or that may have been entered multiple times.

For beginners, it might be best, if it is a recent reconciliation, to undo your previous reconciliation and redo it. Yes, it's a bit more work, but don't you want your books to be accurate? Ideally, after you redo the reconciliation and add or remove the culprit your reconciliation will be ready to go for the current period.

To Resolve the Issue of Missing Transactions

Oftentimes we get busy throughout the month and forget to add a debit we made at the gas station or sales from a certain day. This is normal and happens to the best of us—it is the reason why we reconcile.

You will want to go through your reconciliations, for example with the bank statement, circling items that are missing from your QuickBooks. Then, once you get to the end of the reconciliation using the Find feature in QuickBooks Desktop (Edit » Find) or the search bar in QuickBooks Online, you will want to search for those missing amounts. Maybe you entered them but entered them incorrectly. Perhaps you used the checking account but accidentally said you used cash on hand or vice versa.

If you are out of luck and the transactions are nowhere to be found, then it is likely you missed entering them, so go to your check register and enter the missing transactions. To access your check register for a specific account, merely locate your chart of accounts and double click the account (such as Checking Bank) that is missing the transactions. Now when you reopen your reconciliation window those transactions will be there for you to match to your statements, bringing your totals right where they need to be!

To Resolve the Issue of Transactions from the Wrong Account

We mentioned this a bit earlier, but sometimes when you're in a hurry you may write checks, make deposits, or enter expenses incorrectly within QuickBooks. All this means is that you selected the wrong drop-down when performing a certain activity like one mentioned above. For example, did you enter a checking account expense into your savings account?

To resolve this issue, simply revisit the individual transactions. QuickBooks is great because it has drop-down features that let you select which account you would like to print a check from. If you accidentally selected savings but meant checking, simply select the other account from the drop-down.

If you entered expenses in the wrong account, they are likely located in the wrong register. Simply delete these transactions and reenter them in the correct account. When you reconcile at the end of the month, you know you performed it correctly when everything matches!

Some Other Reconciliation Issues

Mistakenly Clearing Transactions Not on Statement

We all do it, when we are rushing to mark all the transactions on a reconciliation, we sometimes mismark the wrong one. If you can't easily pinpoint which transaction you incorrectly marked, simply start fresh—a bit of a pain, but wouldn't you rather get it right the first time?

Not Marking All Transactions Shown on Statement

Sure we can make the reconciliation balance—selecting nothing ensures a $0 variance. The point of reconciliations is to ensure that all transactions you think occurred actually occurred. Make sure you mark all transactions shown on your statement!

Confirm Beginning Balance

We touched on this a bit above, but when you make a change in a previous period, the beginning balance will be inaccurate. That means you need to pinpoint where you incorrectly made a historical change and repair it.

Confirm Ending Balance

Often in the heat of the moment when we are in a hurry, we may mistype something. This could be shortchanging the ending balance by a mere ten cents or perhaps even a few dollars. This small difference is an easy fix and will always throw off the balance.

Chapter 9

Monthly Close

What Exactly Are You Closing—A Door?

Closing the month is a phrase you've definitely heard before. What in the world does it mean? Why are accountants always so busy the first week of the month? What in the world is going on?

Financial reporting is a valuable tool for all businesses because it helps leaders make sound decisions, and sound decisions move businesses forward. To make strong and confident financial decisions, one must have solid financials to base those decisions on.

The monthly closing process ensures that the books for the previous month are accurate and representative of the business. We will go over a mini checklist, but first you must understand that if you do not have a repetitive proven process to close the books, your financials will be inaccurate.

What Should I Do?

Below is a list of items that need to take place to properly close the month. This list is in no particular order and you should order your list in a way that best suits your business.

Close Posting Periods

After you ensure that all your payables and receivables have been recorded for the period, you should consider the period closed. That means you have entered and sent out all the invoices you are aware of for the period. This should really happen within the first week of the following month. Sometimes you will get invoices for the previous period after the period has been closed, but simply date them the date of the current month and denote in the memo the correct invoice date. Why? Because the previous period is now closed to all payables entries! If you send out financial statements and then continue to add payables and receivables, then the statements you sent out are inaccurate.

Bank Reconciliation

We went into detail earlier about reconciliations, and now you know that to ensure your financials are accurate and true you must reconcile your bank account. So obviously this is part of the closing process and should be done as soon as everything is entered and you have access to your statement.

Loan & Credit Card Reconciliations

All loan amounts on your balance sheet should tie to your most recent statements. If you owe $100,000 at the end of last month, the balance sheet should say the same amount for that date. Credit cards, also a form of loan, should have all their information entered and then reconciled.

Tie Out Sales

Oftentimes QuickBooks will serve as a backup for your POS system or your sales staff. To ensure the information is accurate in the accounting software you should reconcile it against any other record you have for recording sales. For example, if you run a retail shop, you should take your sales report from your POS for the previous month and ensure the sales information is exactly the same in QuickBooks. If you run an ecommerce store, you should take your sales reports from your website. If it isn't the same, you must investigate and resolve the discrepancy!

Other Accounts Reconciliation

Let's say you process credit cards through an outside service and you get money every third day. Hopefully you have set up another receivable account to track this money and ensure you are getting all of it. At the

94

end of every month, accounts like this should be reconciled to ensure they are correct.

The same could be said about items like cash on hand. You want to ensure all your expenditures are true and accurate. If the account does not reconcile, figure out where the cash went. if it was used for a purchase, make sure to record those receipts.

Monthly Accruals

Accruals are needed to ensure that all revenues and expenses are recognized within the correct reporting period, irrespective of the timing of the related cash flows. An accrual is a journal entry that is used to recognize revenues and expenses that have been earned or used within a period.

Under the double-entry bookkeeping system, an accrued expense is offset by a liability, which appears in a line item in the balance sheet. If accrued revenue is recorded, it is offset by an asset, such as unbilled service fees, which also appears as a line item in the balance sheet.

Some popular accruals are payroll and insurance.
For example, an employer pays their employees on the third day of each month for work the employees completed the previous month. The employer can accrue all wages earned for the month on the 31st to ensure the expense is included and the full amount of

the wage expense is recognized for the appropriate period.

Line Item Review

You should know your business inside and out. To ensure that everything is correct and accurate, you should do an in-depth review of your balance sheet and profit and loss statement. Pull these reports within the QuickBooks software and review each line item. Do these income items belong here? Do these expenses belong here? Is this fuel charge for the company vehicle or for the monthly utility at the warehouse? This is a very important step in the financial preparation and monthly close process. Making sure everything is accurate and true at this step will result in fewer headaches down the road.

Not sure how to class something? Well, make sure to shoot your CPA an email because a good CPA knows that helping you now will make his or her life easier in March.

The review should not stop at ensuring each item is classified correctly but should also ensure items are in the correct period. At the end of the month are all the invoices truly for that period? You do not want to have your previous month look horrible and current month look great if that is just not true. Proper accounting should flush out large variances unless that is the nature of your business.

Prepare Financials

Once you are confident with all the transactions across the period you can prepare financial statements. Usually this report is prepared for the previous financial month. It includes the profit and loss statement, balance sheet, and cash flow statement.

Management Review

A good leader ensures that everyone is on the same page. The management review of financials also ensures things just aren't out of place. By reviewing financials with the manager you can ensure that invoices were not slipped by and paid when they shouldn't have been. This ensures that the correct vendors are coded correctly, and it's a great opportunity to get your management team involved.

Close the Period

The last and probably most important step in the monthly close process is ensuring that no one makes changes to the agreed-upon financials after they have been modified for the last time. To do this, simply close the accounting period. This is a simple option in the QuickBooks Desktop under Settings and for QBO users under the Advanced Settings under Company Settings. The period close date should be set to the last day of the previous month, and a password should be set. Generate that password and save it somewhere, but don't share it with your team! If this password is shared with your team, then they can make changes to previous periods where you may have already presented financials.

Create a Checklist!

Every company is different and has different financial needs. The reality is the above checklist may not be inclusive of everything you need to close your month or may have offered a list that is too in-depth. Only you will know what is right for your business and should consult with your CPA if you are not quite sure.

The smoothest way to ensure you cover all the necessary items mentioned above is to create a simple checklist in Excel. Create a checklist with which you start fresh every month, with a section for notes. In the hurry of getting the books closed, you may have forgotten to do something or need to make a change the following month. By reviewing the old checklist prior to the current one you will ensure that issues do not plague you right up until it is time to file taxes and are instead handled in a timely fashion.

How Should I Organize My Month Close?

If you are a stickler for organization, it is recommended that you find a digital place to house all your information. Perhaps place the files on your computer that you back up regularly, a cloud-based storage service, or an external hard drive. This device or service should be organized by year and then month. All your items for, say, June should be stored within that June folder.

With this organization it will be easier to report to investors and share with your accountant and/or business partners. Everything will be closed properly, and any changes you made will be backed up.

Included in this hub should be everything that you marked off the previously mentioned checklist. Everything from your POS reports to your reconciliation of loans. Don't stop there though, include all your loan statements, bank statements, and anything else pertaining to the month. In the world of accounting and keeping a trail, more is always better!

I Have a Checklist for You

Sometimes the first version of a monthly close checklist can be daunting. I went ahead and decided to create one for you. Head over to my website *zacweiner.com* and simply search for "monthly close checklist"—you will be able to easily download an Excel sample version.

Chapter 10

The Wide World of Inventory

Why Should I Care About Inventory?

For any business that retails or produces products, inventory is a lifeblood. Without proper inventory management and controls, the business will never pass the stage of infancy. However, even though inventory is a key component of success, for a small business, it can also be extremely time consuming and costly to maintain. This chapter will serve to balance those two extremes: the importance of proper inventory controls alongside the human capital expense of keeping an accurate inventory.

QuickBooks, as you have learned thus far, is an amazing tool to expedite accounting and bookkeeping management. It allows for many things to be automated, from tracking bank transactions to sending customers automated invoices. Unfortunately, inventory management is likely one of the weakest aspects of the program and the most difficult to learn as a novice accountant and bookkeeper.

What Exactly Is Inventory?

Before we dive into the intricacies of QuickBooks and inventory management, let's understand exactly what inventory is. We have defined this in our key terms chapter as:

Inventory, often called merchandise, is an asset that is intended to be sold in the ordinary course of business.

Inventory gets complicated because it may not be immediately ready for sale. For the sake of your small business, inventory items can fall into one of the following three categories:

1. Goods held for sale in the ordinary course of business; or
2. Goods that are in the process of being produced for sale; or
3. The materials or supplies intended for consumption in the production process.

Most small businesses will fall into the first category. In other words, this means you buy goods from a vendor and then sell them to a customer. These goods have no added value (such as additional components, labor to finish the goods, etc.) or changes applied to them.

Inventory gets even more complicated when multiple components come together. For example you buy part 1 from Vendor A and part 2 from Vendor B. The finished product is the combination of part 1 and part 2 and is then sold to a customer.

Obviously as you think about growing your business from five products to a hundred, this gets overwhelming quickly! No need to stress, though; this chapter can guide you through the basics, highlighting some shortcuts and helping to make you an inventory pro in time for closing your next month's books.

Which QuickBooks Program Does My Business Need?

Which of the above categories did you fall into? Numbers 1, 2 or 3? This will help you define which QuickBooks product is best for your small business.

Do you merely buy and sell products from a vendor to a customer? If you fall under this category, QuickBooks Online and QuickBooks Pro will solve all your problems. Even if you usually sell certain pieces together, the QuickBooks Online grouping tool will help you bundle these together and easily sell them with the click of a button.

Now if you do more than just buy and sell the same product, such as buy multiple pieces from multiple vendors, combining them to get a finished good, you will need a bit more computing power! These more complex combinations are called inventory assemblies and require QuickBooks Premier and higher to accomplish your goals. Unfortunately, at the time of this writing, QuickBooks Online does not have the inventory assembly feature launched quite yet.

Here is a brief overview of the QuickBooks products and their inventory capabilities:

QuickBooks for Mac

For businesses that merely buy and sell products from a vendor to a retail or wholesale customer.

QuickBooks Online

For businesses that merely buy and sell products from a vendor to a retail or wholesale customer.

QuickBooks Pro

For businesses that merely buy and sell products from a vendor to a retail or wholesale customer.

QuickBooks Premier

For businesses that buy, sell, and combine products to retail or wholesale to their customers. This system allows for basic manufacturing, grouping and build of materials.

QuickBooks Enterprise

For businesses that buy, sell, and combine products to retail or wholesale to their customers. This system allows for basic manufacturing, grouping and build of materials. Additionally, it has the most complex

105

manufacturing ability compared to all the QuickBooks products.

How Does Your Business Work?

As you likely know, businesses are not the same. Some businesses manufacture goods. Other businesses buy wholesale and then retail goods. While others may buy multiple goods and combine them to make a finished product. If you are a consultant like myself, you merely exchange time for money and no sale of physical goods takes place.

Knowing which of the following buckets you fall into helps you ensure you focus on the right inventory setup:

Manufacturer

A manufacturer takes raw materials and by hand or machinery creates a product. For the sake of accounting, combining two finished goods to make a new finished good is considered manufacturing because the accounting software must go through the step of combining the goods to have the final good to sell and record the cost of goods.

Wholesale

Wholesale describes companies that buy goods, usually in large quantities (sometimes small to start),

106

and resell them at a higher price. The normal definition of a wholesaler does not generally include the manipulation of the goods from the purchase to resale process.

Retail

A retailer buys finished goods (similar to how a wholesaler operates, but usually in smaller quantities), and then resells the goods on a per unit basis. Retailers do not usually manipulate finished goods and merely resell the unit they bought at a higher price.

New Age Retailer

New age retailers sell products unique to them. This kind of product would have custom packaging and denote the business's brand name (and not, for example, the name of a wholesaler). Some products may come in as a finished good, while others may need finishing. New age retailers play the role of manufacturer from an accounting perspective. They may buy multiple components and combine them to retail a finished good. Additionally, they oftentimes will sell online as well.

Digital Retailers

Digital retailers are similar to new age retailers in that they sell products unique to them. Usually the sale occurs over the internet—think ecommerce store. Oftentimes they also retail finished goods from other vendors. Their core business is online, meaning their inventory is often kept in a remote warehouse or with a fulfillment partner. For example, these products would have custom packaging and denote the digital retailer's brand name. Some products may come in as a finished good, while others may need finishing. Digital retailers play the role of manufacturer from an accounting perspective. They may buy multiple components and combine them to retail a finished good, or they may buy finished goods, making no modification, and resell them.

New Age Wholesaler

New age wholesalers can buy and sell digitally, never holding any inventory. They may buy from one company and sell to another customer, never handling the goods. Often referred to as dropshippers, these businesses need not account for their goods as manufactures since they make no modifications to the products.

Service Business

A service business provides work performed in an expert manner by an individual or team. The typical service business provides intangible products, such as accounting, banking, consulting, cleaning, landscaping, education, insurance, treatment, and transportation services. These businesses usually hold no inventory and their payroll expense is the main cost of sales.

Understanding Cash and Accrual Accounting with Inventory

A key component lots of small business owners miss when setting up their accounting is understanding that the decision to go with cash or accrual accounting deeply affects how inventory is handled. Yes, the decisions you make today affect your future and your tax bill.

Cash

The difference is fairly simple, when on a cash basis, the purchase of inventory is recorded under cost of goods—not on the balance sheet. So, this expense is booked the month you buy the inventory and the cash goes out. For example, you buy 100 widgets in February, and the wholesale price is $5. In your February financials you will see the cost of goods as $500. This holds whether you sell zero units or 25 units because the cost-of-goods expense is recorded the month you bought the goods. In the following months no cost of goods will be recorded if you buy no inventory.

The cash method is very challenging when accounting for inventory in this manner. How do you know what months you made money or lost money? It's almost impossible to tell without doing some additional work.

Accrual

On accrual basis, COGS is recorded when an item is sold. For example, 150 widgets are sold in January, and 150 widgets COGS is recorded in January. This lends itself to more work on a regular basis for accounting purposes but results in more accurate financials. The income statement will show expenses with the correctly related income. In the following months, if 100 or 250 units are sold, the related COGS are recorded in those months.

Inventory in this scenario lives on the balance sheet until the COGS are recorded on the income statement. This brings in another aspect in business accounting: Basically, it means that you can have a profitable quarter but essentially have less cash then before. This is why the statement of cash flows will be very important for you going forward.

Though the accrual method may require a bit more work, the benefits of seeing true income against true expenses and knowing if the business made or lost money will make running a profitable business well worth the work.

How Should You Inventory it?

The type of retailer you are really decides how your inventory system will be set up. There are two main groups of thought on how to treat finished goods and the associated inventorying of those goods:

1. Build of Materials (also known as BOMs)
2. Finished Product SKU

For those of you with complex inventory backgrounds, you will probably point out that a product sku is a variant of build of materials. That is correct, but the key to the above differentiation is that you either have the entire build of materials, with inventory parts and a finalized product SKU, or you just have a finished product SKU.

A majority of digital age retailers buy a finished product either internationally or domestically. The product is produced with all component pieces and then packaged as it would be to ship out the good. Setting up a complex SKU system based on BOMs is merely tedious work that creates no value for anyone on the development, accounting, or management side.

That is true of course only if you do not source product components from various supplies. If you source from multiple suppliers and combine goods to create finished goods, your accounting inventory needs are complex. This means you have to build finished goods within the accounting program—combining goods from Vendor A and Vendor B to make one finished good. This is when BOMs will come in handy, and I recommend going that route.

For the rest of the retailing world that buys one finished good and resells it, your SKUs should be just as simple. They should reflect the fact that the same good is purchased as is sold and that no modifications are needed.

How to Set Up Stock Keeping Units (SKUs)

1. Start SKUs with top-level nomenclature

The first 2–3 digits/characters of each SKU number should represent a top-level nomenclature. This can be a department, product type, or even brand (for a company with sub-brands). With this classification, a quick glance at a SKU number identifies the top-level merchandising group and location of any product you have.

2. Use the middle number series to assign unique identifiers

It's helpful to use the middle section of SKU numbers to assign unique features, such as size, color, item type, subcategory, or whatever feature makes sense when organizing the products you sell.

3. Finish SKU numbers with a sequential number

Using sequential numbering (i.e., 001, 002, 003) for the final series of a SKU number makes set-up easy and also helps you identify older versus newer items in a product line.

Pro Tip

Units often come in different case packs or quantities than will be sold. By merely receiving the inventory in the correct manner of how you inventory it, you can avoid any miscounts. For example, in a situation in which you buy 1 case of widget A, but there are 12 units in each case, merely receive 12 units into inventory rather just 1 case.

Manage Inventory Day to Day

Once you have your items set up and these match the platform you are selling on (meaning, if you sell online, the SKUs in QuickBooks match the SKUs in your online store), you must decide how you want to manage this day to day.

There are a few ways in which to do this:

1. Create invoices for each sale.
2. Create a daily invoice for all daily sales.

3. Record daily sales in a journal entry and then create a weekly or monthly invoice to reconcile inventory.

Create Invoices for Each Sale

If you plan on creating an invoice for each sale, hopefully your items are a high dollar amount, and you have relatively small numbers of daily sales. This process can get very tedious when recording an invoice for each transaction by hand, and I caution against this method unless you plan to automate it.

At this point, as mentioned above, you should have set up items within your QuickBooks program. So you will merely record an invoice (sale) for each transaction that occurs. It is your preference if you would like to create a neutral customer called "Online Store" or have each individual customer within QuickBooks.

Deposits should be made into a holding account, or you could select multiple invoices to deposit to match your daily or bi-daily deposit. Depending on how you process credit cards, checks, or cash will determine how you properly set up this system.

Create a Daily Invoice for All Daily Sales

For those that seek great financials without an intense amount of day-to-day work, I recommend creating a daily invoice to compile all your daily sales. This will ensure both revenue and COGS are captured daily, while at the same time minimizing the tedious work associated with this.

You will merely summarize the sales that happened in a given day—totaling all units sold and using one customer called "Ecommerce Sales." This ensures that COGS is recorded daily and that you can run reports showing your store's performance either daily or weekly and dial down on the financials.

Record Daily Sales in a Journal Entry and Then Create a Weekly or Monthly Invoice to Reconcile Inventory

Known as the shortest and sweetest method of inventory management, you can manage inventory on a very macro level. So if you would like to manage it monthly, you merely create one invoice at the end of the month recording all the net sales of each item, resulting in COGS being recorded on the last day of the month while the monthly income statement accurately reflects COGS for the period.

This method poses challenges in reporting when you want to look at daily or weekly performance. Ideally this method should be used for very small stores or as part of a cleanup process to bring financials up to date.

How to Manage Inventory Month to Month

Proper inventory management has as much to do with what you do within QuickBooks as with what you do outside QuickBooks. Oftentimes small business owners obsess over their invoices, billings, and item SKUs, but really have no idea how much inventory they physically have.

The key difference between successful business owners and failing ones is their ability to manage inventory. This means it is key for them to regularly perform a physical count. That's right, on a regular basis, either weekly or monthly, someone on staff— perhaps even yourself—should go through and hand count the items.

What does this even do?

Great question! Ideally this ensures that the number in QuickBooks matches what is actually taking place in the real world. How horrible would it be if you thought you were making money because you sold 10 bicycles at a profit when in fact 10 more walked out the back door, resulting in a loss! The inventory challenges come from all over: It could be short shipping from a vendor, incorrect entry by the admin staff, or theft somewhere along the supply chain that you then got billed for.

Physical counts take out the guessing game associated with accounting and essentially reconcile your QuickBooks data against real-world data.

This can be performed as easily as picking one day a month when it will be completed, say the first Monday of the month. Take the estimated inventory from QuickBooks, print off this list and then count each physical item to ensure it matches your estimates.

There are plenty more specifics about how to properly track and reconcile inventory that are beyond the scope of the book—the key is that it is performed regularly. What good are financial statements if they are inaccurate?

Inventory can easily be adjusted in both QuickBooks Online and QuickBooks Desktop. The online version requires you to select the plus symbol, go to Inventory Qty Adjustment, and select the items, date, and quantity you would like to adjust. QuickBooks Desktop is a similar process, the option is just located under the inventory module, then select Adjust Quantity/Value on Hand.

> **Pro Tip**
>
> Set up inventory correctly from day one—this will ensure your bookkeeping headache stays at a minimum well into the future.

Chapter 11

How to Properly Perform Simple Daily Tasks

Simple Tasks Are Important Too

One of the most challenging parts of accounting for your small business will be the day-to-day tasks that must be accomplished. This list is long and challenging, but do not fret—you will likely only be using a small part of it.

What Are Customers?

Who are your customers? That is the first step you need to ask yourself. For the purpose of simplifying your books, you should look at customers a bit differently than everyone else. In general, customers are put into two buckets: low average sales price with large volume, and high average sales price with low volume. Those categories are distinctively different and should be treated as such.

Low Volume Sellers

If you have a low volume of customers, you want to add a unique customer for each individual or entity you sell to. You may sell to Company A, Company B, and Company C. You may sell to Large Customer 1, Large Customer 2, and Large Customer 3. Each of these is a different customer group and should be set up separately and invoiced individually.

High Volume Sellers

If you have a high volume of customers, you should not track every sale individually in QuickBooks. You should track overall sales and then denote the receivables by processor. For example, if you have a small online store, you should track sales by your payment processor. An example name is Credit Card Processor A. If you process through multiple banks or multiple processors, you should have Credit Card Processor A and Credit Card Processor B.

What Are Vendors?

Perhaps you are a vendor and know what this means. Or perhaps you buy from multiple vendors every day. Vendors are those who supply goods and services to you. For example, the t-shirts on the rack that you buy from your friend overseas are purchased from your friend the vendor. The nice lady that comes and cleans the office weekly, yes, she too is a vendor. Each check written to this individual or to these firms should be tracked, which allows you to run vendor reports for a specific time.

Pro Tip

Remember to get W-9s from your vendors who supply services or digital goods over $600 on an annual basis. At the end of the year, your tax preparer (or perhaps you) will need to present these individuals with a completed 1099 form. The IRS requires that you disclose who rendered you services and the amounts you paid. Stiff penalties apply for those who do not comply.

How Do I Add and Edit Vendors?

This varies a bit depending on which QuickBooks version you are using. On the desktop versions, you will find this feature on the top navigation bar under Vendors. Once you select the Vendor drop-down, you can either add a new vendor on the drop-down or within the Vendor Center. Remember to add all the necessary information from the tax id to the address, because when you print checks, this will be the address that appears on the printed check!

When you utilize QuickBooks Online, the Vendor option will be on the left side. After you select this, you will see a button on the top right where you can select the New Vendor option. Once you add this, a window will prompt you to enter all the necessary information as mentioned in the above paragraph.

Coding bank feeds will be covered shortly, but once you get all your key vendors set up with the correct name, mailing address, and payment terms, entering bills and coding your bank feeds will be a breeze because everything you need to know about the vendor is right there!

How Do I Enter Bills?

This process will show you how to get bills entered into the QuickBooks accounting software. Obviously this varies a bit between versions, but the core concepts are the same.

If you are using QuickBooks Desktop, you have a quick start button on the home screen that allows you to select Enter Bills. If you want to be one of the cool kids, simply select Vendors from the top navigation bar and then select Enter Bills. For those using QuickBooks Online, simply hit the plus button at the top right of the screen and then select Bill under Vendor.

Where it offers you the option to choose Vendor, you will simply start typing the first few words of the vendor as you would in any autofill software. Once the vendor you are looking for populates, select that one (if it does not yet exist in the system, feel free to add a new vendor).

The next step is what separates the children from the adults. Enter the information from the statement— invoice number, amount due—and then code the invoice. This is where it can get confusing because you want to ensure your invoice is coded correctly so your financials are correct. Let's say you run a retail shop and buy paper. This paper is used for both the shop printers and the office that services your online business. You are meticulous about where your money goes and want to track the two. So you code each of those paper purchases to "office supplies, office" or "office supplies, retail." Make sure your invoice total matches your entered total, and each purchase is coded to the right general ledger code.

If you set up the correct terms and due date, now when you enter the bills, your cash management will be better in the future. This ensures that when you run payables reports, the money and dates you owe vendors will be correct. Remembering the small steps now can save you lots of time in the future.

What Are Checks?

A check is a written, dated, and signed instrument used to make or receive payment. This paper instructs the bank to pay a definite sum of money to a specific individual. For your QuickBooks purposes, you should have checks that can be printed and handwritten checks as well. As you write or print these checks, you should be record them within the QuickBooks system.

How Do I Write Checks?

Automating the check writing process, if you have not yet done so, will blow your mind. The first step in the process is, as outlined above, entering bills in QuickBooks. Once you successfully complete this process you can move on to writing checks.

The second step in this process after entering your bills is selecting the Pay Bills option. This is located on the home screen on QuickBooks Desktop (or under Vendors and Pay Bills) or under the plus button on QuickBooks Online. In this area you can select which bills you would like paid by simply selecting them—you can even search by vendor of choice.

After you select the bills you would like to pay, either select Pay and Print if using QBO or Print Later if using QuickBooks Desktop. These transactions have been entered into the system and will adjust your banking balance, but have yet to be printed.

The third and final step in the check-cutting process is printing these checks. This is located on the home screen for QuickBooks Desktop as Print Checks (or under Vendor and Print Checks) or under the plus sign as Vendor Print Checks in QBO. Simply select the checks you would like to print and enter the starting check number (checks should always go in numerical order).

What Are Bank Feeds?

Bank feeds are simply the transactions that hit your bank account. This is a great feature of the new accounting software that makes the month close process much easier and ensures that all your transactions are properly accounted for (no more double entering transactions or missing a debit charge). Under the banking section of QuickBooks, the software can automatically bring down your transactions without you manually entering them all. These bank transactions appear and allow you to code them as expenses to the correct vendor and associated account.

How to Set Up Bank Feeds?

For QuickBooks Desktop, it is simpler and more cost effective to download your feed from the bank and then upload it into your desktop program. Banks vary in how they let you access this information, but you simply want to download the QBO or QBX file for a specified date range and upload into one of the QuickBooks desktop versions.

Once you have this file saved on your computer, you simply go to the Banking drop-down at the top of your program and select Import Bank Feeds. This is a simple and quick way to get all the data from your bank inside the accounting program. The first time you set this up you will have to map the bank you imported to the bank on your balance sheet. So make sure you upload the transactions to your checking if it is your checking, or to savings if it is your savings. Once you map or select the right account, QuickBooks Desktop will remember it for future uploads.

For QBO users, the process is a bit different. Under the banking section on the left of your online portal, you should go to the main banking screen. Once there, you can select Add a Bank Account to the banking section. It is a simple process where you simply add your online credentials to the system. Once done, you can map the account to the correct account on the balance sheet. Voila! You will see the bank feeds on your banking section. Instead of manually downloading this information each time, you simply select Update Banking and the banking is updated.

Pro Tip

Bank feeds work for both bank accounts and credit cards. Save time and energy by importing all of these accounts using the QuickBooks built-in features.

What Are Bank Feed Rules?

One of the great features of technology is the ability for it to memorize certain actions. QuickBooks bank feeds memorize transactions. For example, do you take your team out for a pizza lunch every Friday? For your convenience, QuickBooks memorizes the name of your pizza place (Pizza Place 1) and the code (meals and entertainment). So every time it sees a transaction from Pizza Place 1 it knows to code it to meals and entertainment.

Pro Tip

Want to figure out what your true cash position is for the day? Make sure you update your banking, then you know your position for today.

Want to know your correct check run for the period? Process your bank feeds and select Print Checks. This ensures that you know if you are overdrawing your account in the check-cutting process.

How to Enter Expenses?

As covered above, one of the key components to managing and entering your expenses will be your bank feeds. The other key component will be manual entry on your end. Perhaps you have a large expense you plan on making tomorrow and want to ensure your cash position is solid. By manually entering this transaction you can ensure that your cash position sustains that kind of purchase. For QuickBooks Desktop, simply enter the Write Checks window, and this will record the expense. For QBO, select the plus sign and Expenses.

For those who want to take it to the next step, you can actually go within the banking register and make adjustments. For example, from the home screen of QuickBooks Desktop, select Check Register to manually add expenses (this is located under Chart of Accounts and the selected register in QBO).

What Is the Item List?

Items are things you buy or sell. These items can be used to generate invoices that you send customers or even to help you enter bills if you wish to track inventory. Item lists help you better organize your invoices by creating items that you use regularly and setting preset prices as well as descriptions

The items can be mapped to COGS or expenses depending on what you are trying to accomplish. Take the simple example of a wholesale coffee business. The items can be set for each of the three major blends you sell and the three sizes associated with it. Now your COGS could be broken out by each blend so you know what your true cost is each time you sell coffee!

Also, with the Item list is the Other Names list. This is where your business owners live because business owners are neither customers nor vendors. Use this other names list to cut distribution checks or keep your owners' equity in order.

What Are the Different Item Types?

Service

This refers to a service you provide to a customer. For example, window cleaning would be a service. This has no tangible transaction, no goods leave one company and go to another company. In other words, you will have no change in your current inventory. The service item type is great for creating services that you can charge by the job or the hour.

Inventory Part

This refers to an item that you purchase with the goal of reselling. An example of this would be a widget. You bought the widget for $5 and will sell it for $15. You want to track this item on your balance sheet and book the COGS when the item sells.

Non-Inventory Part

This is an item that is an inventory piece, but one that you do not wish to track with the QuickBooks program.

Other Charge

Here you would add an item like shipping charge, markups, or other items you would like to appear on invoices.

What Are Sales Receipts?

A sales receipt records a sale and the transfer of money, while an invoice is a receivable to be paid. Oftentimes sales receipts are preferred in situations where a POS is not present, and you want payment to occur on the spot. For example, a customer walks in your shop and wants to buy your artwork. Obviously you won't invoice this brand new customer and hope they pay at a later date. You will bill them now, receive the money, record the sale, and then let them walk out the door with the artwork.

For more complex accounting purposes, sales receipts are also great because they record sales for an entire day when you do not want to enter individual transactions. Did your ice cream shop make 150 sales today? Well, obviously you did not want to create a sales receipt for each sale. You can capture all the sales for the day in your POS and transmit this data by simply entering a sales receipt from the information printout from your POS. By entering this sales receipt in QuickBooks, you now have all the financial information you need in your accounting software that was previously in your POS.

How Do I Make Sales Receipts?

For the purpose of most retail and ecommerce businesses, sales receipts will be a blessing. Instead of making complex journal entries, you can simply open the house vendor you created, such as POS Customers, and create a sales receipt to record the sales on a specific day. Oftentimes sales receipts will have line items for refunds, merchant processors, or even different types of product revenues. Tracking these items ensures that your top line revenue is correct and all the associated fees and refunds are recorded.

To set up the sales items, refunds, and processing fees, you simply visit your item list as previously discussed. Here you can create specific items (services are the best because they don't require inventory adjustments). These items help you track sales receipt items so they hit specific line items on your income statement or balance sheet. It is as simple as selecting them when you set up the item!

How Does Sales Tax Work?

Since this book covers such a broad scope of industries and is available in all states, I am not spending too much time on the topic of sales tax. This is because many nuances occur state to state, city to city, and business to business. Though, for basic accounting purposes one should understand how it works.

Sales tax is technically money the business holds for the government. This means it is not yours, the business's, or your Uncle Joe's. In all states the government is very serious about getting their sales tax and will lock your doors if they do not get it.

Sales tax should sit on the balance sheet until it is paid. It is a current liability and should be reconciled against the point of sale, sales software, or however you record sales on a regular basis.

Chapter 12

Recording Daily Sales

Get a Sales System In Place

Small business owners usually have a system for every aspect of their business but accounting. The majority of the time when I take over accounting for a business or when I bring on a new client, the issues are very similar: These small business owners have failed to set up a basic accounting workflow.

We touched on this a bit in a previous chapter when we talked about getting organized weekly and the importance of setting a weekly schedule. Here we are going to go a bit deeper so that you understand how both accounting and QuickBooks regular activities should be treated.

Invoice and Bill Flow

Often seen as obvious to experienced operators and accountants, this concept is key to any small businesses success. It works as follows:

1. Invoices or bills received
2. Invoice or bill entered into QuickBooks
3. Invoices or bills marked paid in QuickBooks
4. Either print a check, make an online payment, process an expense, or make a credit card payment

Let's take a look at each item individually.

Invoice or Bill Received

It could be as simple as setting up a folder in your inbox to manage these invoices or as complex as having a digital storage folder broken up by vendor. Find a flow-through that works for you but ensures you are receiving all your invoices or bills in one place. This could also be a simple binder where you have physical invoices set to be processed. This will make it easier when you select one day a week to sit down and process those items, which leads us to step two.

Invoices or Bills Entered into QuickBooks

Once all these invoices and bills are in one place, it's easy to sit down and enter them all into QuickBooks (for online users it is as easy as selecting Enter Bills from the top right plus sign). Personally, I find it easiest to alphabetize and then enter by vendor. This creates a quick and clean workflow. Now that you have done the hard part, you can figure out what to do next.

Pro Tip

Take this time to update your banking and cash position, which we will review later. We want to ensure we have sufficient funds to process all necessary checks.

Invoices or Bills Marked Paid in QuickBooks

After deciding which items we want to pay this week, we are going to select them in the Pay Bills section of QuickBooks. We must first know what we want to pay and how we will pay it before starting this step. For example, if you always pay Vendor Bob with a credit card, we will need to process that payment in QuickBooks as such. For checks, we can select Print Later or Print Now and enter the check numbers. Use the Print Later function if you are printing multiple checks, and the Print Now function for handwritten checks; simply enter the check number as you go. This leads us to our next step, or applying the payment.

Print a Check, Make An Online Payment, Process An Expense, or Make Credit Card Payment

There are many ways to make a payment and oftentimes multiple accounts to make a payment from. Ensure that you have decided in advance which items will be paid which way. Then, after processing, as we mentioned above, you will make the final payment by whichever means you decided. If anything changes from what you expected, merely go back and make the change in QuickBooks.

The invoices and bills flow-through is key to any important small business. Most times I see small business owners writing checks every day all over the place, without any idea if they even have the cash to cover this. By sitting down and entering all invoices at once, paying them at once, we can ensure a few things. One, we can ensure they are all accurate—who wants to pay phony bills, right? Secondly, we can ensure we have adequate cash to cover these bills and our payroll at the end of the week. Third, if we process correctly, we can easily reconcile our accounts at the end of the month.

Invoice Flow

Though this process may seem quite simple, it's best we walk through it again just in case. We'll assume you have set up your items (either products, services, etc.). If not, skip back to Chapter 10. It is a simple process but important that you follow the correct steps outlined below:

1. Create the invoice.
2. Fill out the invoice with all the pertinent information.
3. Send the invoice.

Create the Invoice

Hopefully you have a back office system for knowing which customers received which items. Once you have generated the correct items, as outlined in Chapter 10, you will select the customer you would like to invoice under customers and then select

Create Invoice. Depending on if you are using the online or desktop versions, the invoice creation can be done a few different ways. For Desktop users, there is a Generate Invoice option on your homepage; or under Customers, select Create Invoices on the top navigation bar. For QBO users, you can simply select Create Invoice under the plus button in the top navigation bar.

Fill Out the Invoice with All Pertinent Information

Then select the customer you want to invoice. Pick from the list of your current customers or click "add new" to set up a new customer and enter their billing information. Next, choose your invoice date. This can be today, the date your product ships to your customer, the first day of the month for rent billings, etc. The terms will auto-propagate based off of what you previously set up for this customer (this can always be changed on the individual invoice).

QuickBooks will automatically generate the invoice number, so it's best to leave this field alone. Some organizations will have a per customer system, so do feel free to change this.

I always recommend double checking over your invoice before saving. You want to ensure that your item counts and rate look correct; additionally, you want to ensure your total is relative to your expectations. Remember, the more work you do throughout the month, the easier and more accurate your monthly close will be!

Pro Tip

For those who merely invoice the some customers the same item, week after week (or month after month)— just open the previous invoice you sent them and create a copy, updating the date to the date of the most recent shipment or services rendered.

Send the Invoice

Once you generate the invoice, you can decide how you would like to send the invoice to the client. If you are not quite sure how you want to send it, for the meantime, just save and close. This will save it for a later date. One you decide you want to send it, then you can either print, create a PDF, or email your invoice. The emailing feature is pretty sweet as QuickBooks can connect to your web-based email programs to email your invoices. For QBO users, QuickBooks sends through their own website so linking up your email is merely for customers to reply to.

Receiving Payments

If you created an invoice in QuickBooks to record a sale to a customer, at some point you expect to receive payment related to that invoice. Receiving payments is only necessary if you have an open invoice to apply the payment to.

If you receive a payment from a customer and you have not created an invoice in QuickBooks, then you need to generate a sales receipt related to that customer.

Let's take a look at the steps needed to properly process customer payments:

1. Receive payments.
2. Enter customer payment.
3. Confirm payment was applied.

Receive Payments

Navigating to the customer area, we are going to select Receive Payment. I recommend having the check or wire information in front of you. This will ensure you have both the correct dollar amounts and the proper invoices to reference.

Again, double-checking this information now will not only make the next few steps easier, but the entire monthly close process simpler.

Enter Customer Payment

Entering the customer payment has quite a few components, and it is very important that you get these correct. Not handling the following items correctly will result in incorrect accounts payable, statements, a messed-up bank balance, and much more.

Select the correct customer's name from the drop-down. Then select the payment date, which should be the date that you received the payment. After that, select the payment method from the drop-down list. The options are check, cash, or credit card. This is not as important as the following steps but will make it easier to spot future errors.

Next, enter the reference number: for checks this is the check number; for ACH and wires, this is their reference number as well. Next is the key step to all this: selecting where to deposit the funds. Select the bank account, PayPal account, etc. that you will deposit this payment to from the drop-down.

Finally, enter the amount received. This will auto-populate once you select the corresponding invoice in the Outstanding Transactions list. You can also simply enter the amount and then select the corresponding invoices. Then save and close to process this item.

Confirm Payment Was Applied

The last step is to confirm the payment was applied correctly. To do so, enter the customer section of

QuickBooks, visit the customer just referenced above, and ensure the invoice is marked as paid within the system.

For Desktop Users

For QuickBooks Desktop users, the above steps are very similar except for two nuances: To receive payments, go to the top navigation bar, and under Customers select Receive Payments. Additionally, the Make Deposits option is located under the banking navigation tab.

So essentially QuickBooks Desktop has two steps: receiving payments under the customer section and then making the deposit under banking. For those of you who receive numerous deposits daily, ensure you make a single deposit with multiple customer payment receipts. This will make sure your banking goes smoothly.

What Are Sales Journals?

Oftentimes when sales are recorded in another system, such as a Point of Sale, there is a lot of data that needs to be transmitted into QuickBooks. Sales journals help track multiple revenue types with multiple payment processors, allowing you to book complex sales for a given day. Think of a sales journal as a sales receipt on steroids. Instead of going into each sales receipt and processing multiple payment types individually, you set up a sales journal to help you organize all of your payment types in one transaction. For example, if you have multiple profit centers but one payment processor, you want to show on the income statement all the places where the revenue is coming from. Sales journals help you with this process.

How Do I Make a Sales Journal?

Sales journals can get complex quickly, but let's look at a simple journal where you record the sale of goods from your POS. For this example, your POS processes MasterCard and Visa together, separate from American Express. You are going to track your revenue by two revenue types: coffee and ice cream.

4100 – Ice Cream - Credit - $150
4200 – Coffee - Credit - $200
2300 – Sales Tax Payable - Credit $17 (tax rate of 6.5%)
1410 – MasterCard/ Visa Receivable - Debit - $210
1420 – American Express Receivable - Debit - $157

Congrats, you just made your first sales journal! Remember that your debits and credits should also match (equal each other).

Chapter 13

Key Reports, What They Mean and How to Use Them

Let's Talk Reports

Oftentimes business owners get caught up in the nuances of their product or team and forget the bigger picture. Financials and the related key reports let you take a macro look at what is going on in your business with a clear black and white breakdown. Did you make or lose money for the quarter? Did you gain or lose customers for the month? Was your cost of sales higher or lower than last month? And the list goes on.

This chapter will focus on a handful of key reports that are baked into QuickBooks products and that allow you to quickly and clearly see what is going on in your business.

How to Pull Reports in QuickBooks

Depending on which QuickBooks you are using—Online or Desktop—pulling reports will vary.

For users using QBO, reports are fairly obvious. Located on the left side of the screen, three items up from the bottom you will see the menu option labelled Reports. Once you enter this realm of reports you can pull the basis for all the reports mentioned below, though sometimes the below items may need modifications.

For users using QuickBooks Desktop, finding reports is similarly easy and is located on the top navigation bar three items over from the left. Here, reports are organized by different types, such as sales, financials and reporting, and so on. Similarly, this will be the basis for the reports outlined below.

Monthly, Quarterly, and Annual Reporting

Profit and Loss Statement

This statement is an overview of the income and expenses for a period of time. I recommend looking at the monthly view, quarterly view, and then the quarterly broken out in the monthly format. By reviewing against previous months, you will ensure that you see any anomalies that need to be brought to your attention. Additionally, you can quickly see if the business performance is on track and what recent initiatives are succeeding or failing.

The profit and loss statement shows income earned under the accrual method. It will show all invoices that have been issued, sales recorded, journals entered, and so on. These items will be included even if there are no cash expenditures or money received for them. So even though you have recorded an invoice, you may not have been paid for it yet.

Many business owners confuse the profit and loss profitability with cash the business has made: It is possible to show profits and have reduced cash flow in the same period, unless your business is totally run on a cash basis. This report shows you whether you are making money or not based on the activity of the business during the period.

Keep an Eye On These Items:

1. Review top line income because this measure most directly affects net income.
2. Review cost of goods sold (or cost of sales) to review margins.
3. Review net income (as a total number and percentage of sales).

Balance Sheet

The balance sheet shows a financial picture of a business at a specific day in time. It runs down the assets (what the company owns), its liabilities (what it owes), and the difference between those two, or the company's equity. Some key line items on the balance sheet include: cash, accounts receivable, inventory, accounts payable, and (if you have debt), the portion of long-term debt that is due this year and the balance of any short-term loans (usually secured by accounts receivable and inventory).

You can quickly get the feeling for the health of the business by comparing current assets to current liabilities. For example, do you owe more in accounts payable than you have in receivables and cash? Is so, you have a problem! The balance sheet allows you to see what you owe against what you have very quickly, highlighting pain points before they occur.

Over time, a comparison of period ending balance sheets can give a good picture of the financial health of your business. In conjunction with other financial statements, it forms the basis for sophisticated analysis of your business. The balance sheet is also a tool to evaluate a company's current flexibility and liquidity.

Keep an Eye On These Items:

1. Review large changes in Asset and Liabilities.
2. Calculate and track your current ratio (Current Ratio = Current Assets / Current Liabilities).
3. Calculate and track the quick ratio (Quick Ratio = Current Assets − Inventory / Total Current Liabilities).
4. Calculate and track working capital (Working Capital = Total Current Assets − Total / Current Liabilities).

Statement of Cash Flows

This is a summary of money received and payments made during the period. This may include investing activities as well as financing activities. In layman's terms this means that if you borrowed money, accrued expenses, distributed money to partners, paid sales tax, and so on, these items will be highlighted in this report. I find the statement of cash flows the most insightful report in this section.

By showing what is happening in the cash position today, this month, or last quarter, you can see the pain points in the business. For example, are net profits strong but owner's distributions too high? Are accounts receivable continuing to grow month after month? Is the business profitable but inventory continuing to grow? Lots of insight can be taken from this short report.

Keep an Eye On These Items:

1. Aim for a positive cash flow from operations.
2. Keep a close eye on accounts receivable (hint: it shouldn't be growing unless your business is substantially growing).
3. Plan ahead for cash crunches.
4. Growing inventory should mean growing sales. If not, adjust quickly.
5. Understand the difference between profit and cash, and—more importantly—what is causing the divergence

Cash Flow Projections

This is an estimate of the upcoming cash flow for the future. The projection should be for two to three upcoming months and then be broken out week by week. This report is challenging to compile as it requires taking educated guesses on when you will receive payment on your invoices. Regular expenses and loan payments and other commitments are easier to plot in weekly based on their due dates. This report is vital as it shows whether you have sufficient funds to pay future obligations. If there is a shortfall, knowing when and how to anticipate a proper reaction is key, and this projection will give you the insight to be proactive versus reactive.

Keep an Eye On These Items:

1. Ensure monthly cash in is greater than cash out.
2. Make management decisions based on the projection (don't overbuy when you will be low on cash, cut back payroll if necessary, etc.).
3. Increase capital expenditure or investment if you have significant increasing cash flow.

Daily, Weekly, or Bi-Weekly Reporting

Daily Sales

Understanding what is happening in your business on a daily and weekly basis is the key for any business owner's long-term success. One of the reports I recommend to aid this is the daily sales report. This could come directly from the point of sale or could simply be the invoices generated daily (found under transaction list by customers for one specific day).

153

Either way, understanding the sales flow of your business will help you spot trends before they become an issue.

One of my favorite examples of this is the retail store that is open seven days a week. Every Monday sales are abysmal, 1/20th of a normal day in sales. The owner sees this trend for a month, realizes they are spending more money on labor every Monday than gaining in sale, and decides to close for Monday, which drives more revenue to the bottom line every month into the future.

Keep an Eye On These Items:

1. Daily income
2. Profit center percentage of total

Daily Labor Analysis

For businesses both physical and digital, the daily labor expense is key to mapping out a successful future. I can list all the other types of businesses that necessitate knowing labor cost, like manufactures, services, and so forth, but you already knew your labor cost was important, right?

This analysis is a simple report that maps out what your labor cost is by department or profit center and shows key expenses. Don't forget to include your salaried and management employees because the business still needs to pay for them, too.

By reviewing this item daily, you can see the relevant fluctuations and how they impact your business. Even if your business remains consistently steady, you can ensure that you are making a strong profit by adding this into your daily review. Using this report in conjunction with your daily sales will help you figure out your labor margin, which is key for labor intensive businesses or even those with a large overhead management.

Keep an Eye On These Items:

1. Daily expenses
2. Department percentage of total
3. Fixed and variable percentage of total

Weekly Flash Report

As I highlighted earlier in the chapter, the profit and loss report highlighting company profitability for a period of time is a key report for knowing more about your businesses performance. What if I said that same report could be broken out weekly? That's right, the weekly flash report mimics your regular profit and loss statement but helps you keep tabs on your business on a weekly basis. Though this report may not be one hundred percent precise due to monthly invoices or accruals, you will likely get a strong feel for what is happening week to week.

By reviewing key items from week to week, you can see if items like labor, sales, and other controllable expenses are falling in line. This report also gives you the ability to address things before the month is out and make key changes before any problems spiral out of control.

Keep an Eye On These Items:

1. Weekly profitability
2. Operating margins
3. Week-over-week operating margins

Weekly Unpaid Bills Report

Knowing who you owe and how much you owe them is as important as knowing where and how much in sales has been generated. Hopefully you are entering invoices on a weekly basis, as referenced in a few other places within this book. If not, you should start.

Once all the invoices are entered, perhaps even before you make your weekly check run, review your unpaid bills report! This report will show all vendors, relevant invoices, and what is owed on those invoices.

This report is more important than most business owners realize, for one simple reason: Reviewing this report allows you to be proactive. In layman's terms, you can see what you owe in advance. Instead of realizing that today you owe Vendor A $50,000 and Vendor B $50,000 and have $10 in the bank, you see those expenses weeks in advance and can manage your cash flow properly to avoid that situation. The Weekly Unpaid Bills report allows you to be proactive versus reactive, which is the mark of a successful business owner.

Keep an Eye On These Items:

1. Week-over-week increase or decrease
2. Current liquidity

Weekly Accounts Receivable Report

As important as knowing what you owe is knowing who owes you money. My first thought was to tell the small retail-based business owners to disregard this, but just as important as accounts receivable is knowing when your next processor deposit is coming.

Keeping a finger on the pulse of who owes you money is the key to managing your cash flow. This ensures that you know when money is coming in and you know when to apply leverage to ensure that you keep overdue accounts current. Additionally, it allows you to react quickly to long-time customers who are behind and to easily send a note about overdue amounts.

Effective management of accounts receivable will have direct positive impacts on your cash flow. Essentially, accounts receivable is money that just needs to be turned into cash. The quicker you turn it into cash the better your business cash flow. So focus on this weekly to ensure you are ahead of the curve.

Keep an Eye On These Items:

1. Week-over-week increase or decrease
2. Overdue accounts and their current balance

Chapter 14

Not Goodbye But A See You Soon

All's Not Lost

Entrepreneurs and small business owners are challenged from all sides the first moment their ideas are put into motion. These individuals are truly the Jacks of all trades and the Kings and Queens of wearing many hats. The goal of this book is to make you more confident in wearing the small-business accounting hat.

At the beginning of this journey, we covered the basic terminology and chart of accounts. We then went on to the fundamentals and logic of setting up a weekly schedule and properly closing the month. We wrapped up by touching on some key terms and simple concepts such as bank feeds, inputting expenses, and cutting checks.

Overall, you now have the tools you need to get started on your accounting journey or better do what you are already accomplishing. Remember, the key to long-term accounting success (and business success) is to *always* ask questions. There are plenty of supplementary accounting resources in addition to this book, and you can always reach out to me directly to get more in-depth guidance. Stay hungry my fellow entrepreneurs.

A toast to your financial success.

Stay Up To Date

Be on top of the most recent accounting and small business concepts by visiting my blog at *zacweiner.com*. I send out weekly emails with free collateral, resources, and tools to better run your business.

About the Author

Zachary Weiner began his startup journey at UNC Chapel Hill by partnering with a group of entrepreneurs to change the way online sports lessons were delivered. Upon graduating, he went on to lead marketing at a boutique commercial real estate firm out of New York. Seeing firsthand how transactions occurred, he became interested in finance and turnaround real estate.

Zac spent the next years working his way up to Regional Director at a commercial real estate firm through developing and executing business strategy, operating plans, and budgets. Utilizing a hands-on management strategy, realigning key team members, implementing operational and financial accountability/procedures, Zac was able to see a direct $500k turnaround in less than one year's time from an underperforming entity. Zac's worldview, solid financial knowledge, and grit contributed to his success at the investment firm, leading to his management of multiple properties with a team of hundred, including eight direct reports.

Wanting to get back to the Big Apple, Zac took an opportunity to serve as CFO of a growing restaurant group with 15 locations throughout Manhattan and Brooklyn. There, he took a twenty-first century view of the accounting department: streamlining processes, using technology as a partner, revamping accounting systems, and ensuring proper cash management. He instituted a central treasury program to maximize cash flow and developed a cohesive operating budget. By spending a considerable amount of time working with the operations staff and analyzing the big data, Zac was able to phase out underperforming stores, realign operational hours, and increase overall profits for the parent company.

Zac left the fast casual group in early 2017. Since then, Zac has been an outsourced financial controller and CFO for startups and small businesses across the country. His clients vary from fundraising/pre-revenue to $20 million in annual sales. Through his multiple bestselling books and guides, he has been able to help thousands of small business owners better manage their finances.

Getting in Touch

If you'd like to know when my next book comes out and want to read similar writing every week, sign up at www.zacweiner.com for my mailing list.

Interested in getting some honest and candid feedback about your business finances? Feel free to email me at zac@zacweiner.com or visit the **Work With Zac** section on my website.

If you found anything in this book remotely valuable, there are two ways you could give me a thanks. First, refer this book to a friend who you think will find it beneficial. Second, give me a heartfelt review on the web or social media.

92337225R10097

Made in the USA
Middletown, DE
08 October 2018